BOOTED AND SPURRED

An English sun was shining bright, And English meadows green and gold Were all a-glitter in the light.

G. J. WHYTE MELVILLE : *Lost.*

BOOTED AND SPURRED

AN ANTHOLOGY OF RIDING

Edited and illustrated by

PETER BIEGEL

LONDON
ADAM AND CHARLES BLACK

FIRST PUBLISHED 1949
BY A. AND C. BLACK LTD.
4, 5 AND 6 SOHO SQUARE
LONDON W.I

MADE IN GREAT BRITAIN
PRINTED BY MORRISON AND GIBB LTD., LONDON AND EDINBURGH

To

MR. LIONEL EDWARDS

to whose idea this book
owes its origin

In humble dedication and very
grateful appreciation of all
that I have learnt
from him

EDITOR'S NOTE

The contents of this book have been selected to cover most aspects of the equestrian field. The extracts have been chosen with a view to interest, amuse, and possibly instruct in some small measure, so that they may appeal to both the old and knowledgeable, as well as the young and enthusiastic.

The scope of a book of this kind is necessarily limited. I have tried to find extracts that are less well known than others, and I hope that readers will forgive me if they do not find their own particular favourites which they may think should have been included under the various headings.

P. B.

CONTENTS

ACKNOWLEDGMENTS

I HAVE to acknowledge with grateful thanks permission from authors and publishers of copyright works to include extracts from the following :—

Breaking and Riding by James Fillis, published by Hurst & Blackett Ltd. ; *Conversation Piece* by M. J. Farrell, published by W. Collins, Sons & Co. Ltd. ; *Count Moritz Sandor :* Notes by Leo Singer from *Riding* ; *Crimea* by C. E. Vulliamy, published by Jonathan Cape, Ltd. ; *Donoghue Up !* by Steve Donoghue, published by W. Collins, Sons & Co. Ltd. ; *A Famous Foxhunter : Reminiscences of the late Thomas Assheton Smith* by E. Eardley-Wilmot, published by Sampson Low, Marston & Co. Ltd. ; "Training" by H. S. Persse and "Jockeyship" by F. Fox, from *Flat Racing* in the Lonsdale Library, published by Seeley, Service & Co. Ltd. ; *The Flying Parson and Dick Christian* edited by Major Guy Paget, published by Edgar Backus ; article by Hugh McCausland from *The Horse*, formerly published by the British Horse Society ; *Horse-Sense and Horsemanship of To-day* by Major-General Geoffrey Brooke, C.B., D.S.O., M.C., published by Constable & Co. Ltd. ; *Hunting the Fox* by Lord Willoughby de Broke, published by Constable & Co. Ltd. ; *Maryland and the Grand National*, an article by Noel Laing, published by Polo Magazine Inc. ; *Memoirs of a Fox-hunting Man* by Siegfried Sassoon, published by Faber & Faber Ltd. ; *Modern Pigsticking* by General Sir Alexander Wardrop, G.C.B., C.M.G., published by Macmillan & Co. Ltd. ; *Mount and Man* by Lieut.-Colonel M. F. McTaggart, published by Country Life Ltd. ; *Riding* by Robert Weir ; *Race Riding* by A. E. T. Watson (both in the Badminton Library) and *Hands and Seat* by Robert Weir, published by Longmans Green & Co. Ltd. ; *Saddles Again* by W. H. Ogilvie, published by Gerald Duckworth & Co. Ltd. ; *Squire Osbaldeston : His Autobiography* edited by E. J. Cumming, published by John Lane, The Bodley Head Ltd. ; *The Story of a Red Deer* by the Hon. J. W. Fortescue, published by Macmillan & Co. Ltd. ; *Tschiffely's Ride* by A. F. Tschiffely, published bv William Heinemann Ltd.

Every effort has been made to trace authors or owners of copyright. If, however, I have failed here and there in my search I should like to ask the forgiveness of those concerned for the use of those extracts which I have borrowed without consent.

My personal thanks are due to J. A. Allen of Messrs. J. A. Allen & Co., for giving me the benefit of his knowledge and putting his library at my disposal, and to Messrs. Truslove and Hanson, Clifford Street, W.1., for the loan of several books.—P.B.

PRELIMINARY

Among the various pursuits of man, for his amusement and recreation, that of Riding on Horseback seems to claim the pre-eminence with those whose circumstances afford them the means of opportunity. And this preference is not to be wondered at, when we consider the pleasure, amusement, and benefit we derive from it. For, besides being conveyed wherever our business or inclination requires, the eye is uninterruptedly amused with the objects that pass or surround us ;—a beautiful landscape, or delightful view, are continually presenting themselves.—And, as you like, you may enjoy yourself in contemplation, or your friend in conversation. With all this you receive the benefit of the purest air, so congenial to health, without the least danger of taking cold, or receiving injury, which is prevented by the bodily exercise, of which you take such proportion as your strength will permit, or your inclination, or constitution requires.

John Adams, Ridingmaster : *Analysis of Horsemanship*, 1799.

That riding is the most wholesome of all exercises, I have little doubt. Despite of all the vile stuff that finds its road down his throat who ever heard of a bilious post-boy.

Nimrod : *The Horse and the Hound*, 1832.

Boot, saddle, to horse, and away !

ROBERT BROWNING : *Boot and Saddle.*

I will not change my horse with any that treads but on four pasterns. *Ça ha !* he bounds from the earth as if his entrails were hairs ; *le cheval volant,* the Pegasus, *qui a les narines de feu !* When I bestride him I soar, I am a hawk : he trots the air ; the earth sings when he touches it ; the basest horn of his hoof is more musical than the pipe of Hermes.

He's of the colour of the nutmeg.

And of the heat of the ginger.

It is a beast for Perseus : he is pure air and fire ; and the dull elements of earth and water never appear in him, but only in patient stillness while his rider mounts him : he is indeed a horse ; and all other jades you may call beasts.—It is the prince of palfreys ; his neigh is like the bidding of a monarch, and his countenance enforces homage.—Nay, the man hath no wit that cannot, from the rising of the lark to the lodging of the lamb, vary deserved praise on my palfrey : it is a theme as fluent as the sea ; turn the sands into eloquent tongues, and my horse is argument for them all ; 'tis a subject for a sovereign to reason on, and for a sovereign's sovereign to ride on ; and for the world,—familiar to us and unknown,—to lay apart their particular functions and wonder at him. I once writ a sonnet in his praise, and began thus : *Wonder of Nature* !—

SHAKESPEARE : *King Henry V.*

BUYING A HORSE

OATHS are but words, and words but wind.

SAMUEL BUTLER.

All is gas and gaiters.

CHARLES DICKENS: *The Gentleman in the Small Clothes.*

As mortar sticketh between stones, so sticketh fraud between buyers and sellers of horses.

OLD WRITER.

A horse-dealer is one who reads horses, and understands all the virtues and vices of the whole species. He makes his first application to a horse, as some lovers do to a mistress, with special regard to eyes and legs. He has more ways to hide defects in horse-flesh than women have decays in faces, with which oaths and lies are the most general accompaniments. He understands the chronology of a horse's mouth most critically, and will find out the year of his nativity by it as certainly as if he had been at the mare's labour that bore him; and he is a strict observer of saint-days, only for the fairs that are kept on them—

SAMUEL BUTLER: *Hudibras*, c. 1650.

"'O who shall counsel a man in the choice of a wife or an 'oss?' asked that inspired writer, the renowned Johnny Lawrence. 'The buyer has need of a hundred eyes, the seller of but one,' says another equestrian conjuror. Who can take up an 'oss book and read 'bout splints, and spavins, and stringalts, and corns, and cuttin', and farcy, and dropsy, and fever, and thrushes, and grease, and gripes, and mallenders, and sallenders, and ring-bones, and roarin', etcetera, etceterorem, without a shudder lest such a complication of evils should fall to his lot? Who can expect a perfect 'oss, when he sees what an infinity of hills they are heirs to? . . .

"'Eavens, wot a lot of rubbish has been written about 'osses!" continued the worthy lecturer, casting up his eyes.

"I took a fut rule t'other night and measured off a whole yard and an 'arf of real downright 'ard printin' on the single word 'oss; each succeedin' writer snubbin' the last, swearin' he know'd nothin', until one would expect to arrive at the grand climax of hignorance, instead of gleaning wisdom as one went. . . ."

"At an American 'oss sale I read of t'other day, a buyer exclaims—

"'Vy, he's broken knee'd!'

"'Not at all, you mister,' cried the hauctioneer pertly, 'The gen'leman wot sells this 'oss always marks his stud on the knee, that he may know 'em again'"—haw! haw! haw! chuckled Mr. Jorrocks; "'Lofty hactioned 'oss!—struck his knee again his tooth!' I once heard a dealer declare on behalf of a broken'kneed 'un in the city. . . ."

"There's an old sayin' that it's easier to perceive the wrong than pursue the right; and I reckon it's a vast easier to tell a man wot he should not buy than what he should. . . ."

" No fut, no 'oss."

" When three men enter a yard, a dealer seldom opens out. Two are plenty for business—if the buyer is pea-green, he had better get some riper friend to play first fiddle, and he must be spectator. If he has a button at his 'at, and 'olds his tongue, he may pass for a quiet fox-'unter and so command respect. There's ' masonry ' in fox-'unting, and a loop in at the linin', or a button behind, will do more than all the swagger and bluster in the world.

" It is an inwariable rule with the dealers to praise the bad points and let the good 'uns speak for themselves. It is a waste of time observin' that an 'oss is large in the 'ead or light in the carcase, 'cause a contradiction is sure to follow—It is equally useless axin' the age of a dealer's 'oss because they are all ' six h'off.' If you object to shape, make, or colour, they will tell you it's all fancy ! That some folks like a happle, others a honion, and Lord So-an-so would give any price for sich an 'oss. As to hargufying with a dealer, that's quite out of the question, because he has his cut-and-dried answers to every observation you can make, and two or three grums to swear to what he says. Keep, therefore, in mind what Gambado said about being *done*, keep also in view the sort of nag you want, and don't be talked into buying a cow ; and when an 'oss of your figure makes his appearance, look him full in the face, as though you were used to such interviews. If you have read about sand cracks, and sallenders, and sit-fasts, and thorough pins, and quittors, and locked jaws, and curbs, you will save yourself the trouble of inquirin' after any of them by axin' the dealer if he'll warrant him sound. In course he'll say yes, and you may then proceed with your view. The precept, ' No fut, no 'oss,' is well to be borne in mind, perhaps, as also ' No 'ock, no 'unter.' Now ark forward ! "

ROBERT SMITH SURTEES : " Mr. Jorrocks's Sportin' Lector,"
Handley Cross, 1854.

He hath a good judgement who doth not rely on his own.
OLD PROVERB.

HOW IT SHOULD BE DONE!

" Father," said they, " Tom Kenny is here with a horse——"

" Well I have no time to waste looking at the horse Tom Kenny peddles around the county. What sort is it ? "

" Oh, a common brute," said Willow, with indifferent decision. " The man only came over to see you about the fox covert in Lyran."

" Well, if you say it's a common brute, there's some hope of seeing a bit of bone and substance about the horse. If *you* don't like him, he may be worth looking at." Sir Richard advanced into the yard, and I, following him, caught just the edge of the perfectly colourless wink that passed between his son and daughter. The match of their guile being now well and truly laid to the desired train, they proceeded carelessly on their way. A minute later the two terriers, a guilty pig-bucket look about them, hurried out of the yard in pursuit.

Inside the archway I paused. I love stables and horses and grooms, the cheerful sound of buckets, the heady smell of straw, the orderly fussiness of a saddle-room ; always the same, and ever different. The mind halts, feeling its way into gear with a new set of values at the moment when one sets foot within a stable-yard. The stables at Pullinstown had been built for a larger stud than lodged there now. More than a few doors were fastened up but there was still a stir and a movement about some of the boxes. A lean old hunter's head looked quietly out across the half-door of his box, hollows of age above his eyes, the stamp of quality and bravery on him unmistakably. Next door the shrill voice of the very young complained against this new unknown discipline—the sweat of the breaking tackle still black on an untrimmed neck. A bright bay three-year-old this was, full of quality, and would be up to fourteen stone before he was done with. Such a set of limbs on him too. Bone there you'd be hard to span.

" That's the sort," said Sir Richard, nodding at him. " Ah, if I was twenty years younger I'd give myself a present of that horse. Go back to your stables, I'd say ; I'll never sell you. Good-Day and Romance are over there. I sold a couple of horses last week. Now listen—I hate to sell a horse that suits the children ; but they must go—make room for more—this place is rotten with horses. Well, Tom "—he craned round to a small dark man who appeared quietly from the black mouth of the saddle-room door—" did ye get that furze stubbed out of the hill yet ? " " B'God I did, Sir. Now look-at, the torment I got on the hill of Lyran there's no man will believe. I'm destroyed workin' in it. A pairson wouldn't get their health with them old furzy pricks in their body as thick as pins in a bottle. And then to say five pounds is all the hunt should give me for me trouble ! I'm a poor man, Sir Richard, and a long backwards family to rare, and a delicate dying brother on the place."

" Did Dr. Murphy give you a bottle for him ? " Sir Richard interrupted the recital. " I told him he should go see poor Dan last week."

" Ah, he did, he did, Sir. Sure, then the bottle the doctor left played puck with him altogether, though indeed the doctor is a nice quiet man, and he had to busht out crying when he clapped an eye on poor Dan. He was near an hour there with him, going hither and over on his body with a yoke he had stuck in his two ears. Indeed he was very nice, and Dan was greatly improved in himself after he going. Faith, he slapped into the bottle o' medicine, and he'd take sup now and sup again till—be the holy, I'll not lie to ye, Sir,—whatever was in the bottle was going through him in standing leps. I thought he'd die," Tom Kenny concluded with a pleasant laugh.

"Did he take the dose the doctor ordered?" Sir Richard's long, knotted fingers were crossed before him on the handle of his walking-stick. His head was bent in grave attention to the tale. What, I wondered, of Tom Kenny's horse? And, what, again, of his brother?

"Is it what poor Doctor Murphy told him?" A pitying smile appeared for a moment on Tom Kenny's face. "Well, I'll always give it in to the doctor, he's dam nice, but sure a child itself'd nearly know what good would one two teaspoons do wandering the inside through of a great big wilderness of a man the like o' poor Danny. Sure he drank down what was in the bottle, o' course, and that was little enough for the money, God knows." "Ah, psha!" Impossible to describe the mixture of anger and hopeless tolerance in Sir Richard's exclamation. "Well"—he lifted his head, stabbing at the ground with the point of his walking-stick—"I suppose it's to pay funeral expenses you're trying to sell the horse."

"Now God is my witness, Sir Richard, if I was to get the half o' what this young horse is worth, it'd be more money than poor Danny'll ever see at his funeral or any other time in his life."

"Ah, have done chatting and pull out the horse till I see what sort he is." Sir Richard bent to the match in his cupped hands. Following on this, Tom Kenny retired into a distant loose-box, from which there issued presently sounds of an encouraging nature, in voices so varied as to suggest that a large proportion of the male staff of Pullinstown had assembled in the box.

"Stand over, Willy. Mind out would he split ye!"

"Go on out you, Tom, before him."

"Sure every horse ye'll see rared a pet is wayward always."

"Well, now isn't he the make and shape of a horse should have a dash of speed?"

Is it them Grefelda horses? Did ye ever see one yet wasn't as slow as a man?"

"Well, he's very pettish, Tom. What way will ye entice him?"

"*Hit him a belt o' the stick!*" came with sudden thunder from across the yard where Sir Richard still stood. Whether or not his advice was acted upon, a moment later the Grefelda horse shot like a rocket out of the stable door, his owner hazardously attached to his head by a single rein of a snaffle bridle.

" Woa-boy-woa the little horse." Tom Kenny led him forward, nagging him to a becoming stance with every circumstance of pompous ownership.

I am a poor enough judge of a horse in the rough, but this one seemed to me to have the right outline. There was here a valuable alliance of quality and substance, and as he was walked away and back to us, a length of stride promising that he should gallop.

" That'll do," said Sir Richard, after a prolonged, sphinx-like inspection. " I'm sorry to see he plucks that hock, Tom ; only for that he's not a bad sort at all. Turn him around again. Ah, a pity ! "

" May God forgive yer honour," was Tom Kenny's pious retort ; " ye might make a peg-top o' this horse before ye'd see the sign of a string-halt on him. Isn't that right, Pheelan ? " He appealed to a small man with a wry neck and a surprising jackdaw-blue eye, who had stood by throughout the affair in a deprecating silence, unshaken even by this appeal.

" What height is he ? Sixteen hands ? " Sir Richard stood into the horse.

" Sixteen one, as God is my judge," corrected the owner. " Well, now," he compromised, as Sir Richard remained unshaken, " look—he's within the black of yer nail of it."

Even at this distance I judged, after a glance at Tom Kenny's outstretched thumb, it would leave him no more than a strong sixteen. However that might be, I more than liked the horse, and so I rather suspected did Sir Richard, the more when I saw him shake his head and turn a regretful back to the affair.

" Sir Richard,"—Tom Kenny's head shot forward tortoise-like from his coat collar—" look-at—eighty pounds is my price—eighty pounds in two nutshells."

" Well, Tom," Sir Richard smiled benignantly, " I'm always ready to help a friend, as you know." He paused, his head bent again in thought, " Now if I was to ride the horse, and that is to say if I *like* this horse, I wouldn't say I mightn't give you sixty-five pounds for him," came with sudden generous resolve.

" May God forgive you, Sir," Tom Kenny turned from the pious suggestion with scarcely concealed horror. Tears loomed in his voice as he continued in rapt encomium, " Don't ye know yerself ye might do the rounds o' the world before ye'd meet a horse the like o' that ! This horse'll sow and he'll plough and he'll sweep the harvest in off o' the fields for ye. Look-at!" (with sudden drama). "If ye were to bring this horse home with ye to-day, ye mightn't have a stick o' harvest left standing to-morra night. And he'll be a divil below a binder."

"Faith, true for you, Tom Kenny. That one's very lonely for the plough," Pheelan of the jackdaw eyes struck in with irresistible sarcasm. "Sure, it's for Master Dick to hunt him the Sir'll buy him." Without a change of expression, Tom Kenny tacked into the wind again. "Well, ye'd tire three men galloping this horse, and there's not a ditch in the globe of Ireland where ye'd fall him," said he with entire and beautiful conviction.

"Ah, have done. Get up on him, you, Pheelan, and see would you like him." Sir Richard spoke with brief decision.

Following on this the prospective purchase was ridden and galloped into a white lather by Pheelan, whose hissed "Buy him, sir; he's a *topper*!" I overheard as Sir Richard prepared to mount, and having done so, whacked the now most meek and biddable horse solemnly round the yard with his walking-stick, before he changed hands for the sum of sixty-eight pounds, a yearling heifer, and thirty shillings back for "luck."

"And damned expensive, too," said my cousin as, the deal concluded, we pursued our way onwards to look at the young horses; "only I hate bargaining and talking I'd have bought him twice as cheap. . . . Isn't that a great view? You should paint that. I would if I was an artist."

We had walked up a hilly lane-way, splitting a flock of sheep driven by a young lad as we went. The river lay low on our right hand now. Everywhere the gorse shone like sweet gold money, and primroses spread pale lavish flames.

The whole air was full of a smoky gold light. It lay low against the rose of the ploughed fields. It was weighted with the scent of the gorse. The young horses were splendidly bathed in light. They grouped themselves nobly against the hillside before they swung away from us, with streaming manes and tails, to crest the hill like a wave, and thunder away into the evening. Nor, though we stayed there an hour, could we get near them again. My cousin at last exasperated led me back to the house and dinner.

M. J. FARRELL: *Conversation Piece.*

People talk about size, shape, shoulders, quarters, blood, bone, muscle, but for my part give me a hunter with brains, he has to take care of the biggest fool of the two and think for both.

G. J. WHYTE MELVILLE: *Riding Recollections.*

" Buy him, sir ; he's a topper ! "

A HISTORICAL HORSE DEAL

When Alexander was a young man a horse dealer called one day at Philip's court and offered a very beautiful horse for sale. It was a big, upstanding black horse, only half broken, with a white blaze or star, the shape of a bull's head. The king liked the look of the animal and told his head groom to try it out, but no sooner had he mounted than the horse started to rear and buck and the rider came off. Several others tried to ride it, but no one succeeded to stay on. Then the young Alexander begged his father to allow him to have a try, and the king agreed.

Alexander had noticed that the horse had stood all the time with his quarters towards the sun and had got upset by his own and the rider's shadow facing it, so he started by turning the horse round so that it faced the sun. He began by patting and quietly talking to it, and then slowly mounted. The horse, although still fidgety and nervous, behaved much better and started off at a walk, then broke into a trot and then a canter at which Alexander kept it for some time, going round in a wide circle, so that when gradually the sun got behind, the horse took no notice of the shadow.

When Alexander finally returned and dismounted, his father was so pleased at his son's performance that he bought the horse and made a present of it to the boy, who became greatly attached to it, and broke it in himself. He gave it the name of Bucephalus, which is the Macedonian word for Bull's Head, referring to the shape of the star on the horse's forehead.

Bucephalus carried Alexander through all his battles during his famous campaign, got wounded several times like Alexander himself, and finally died on the banks of the River Hydaspes in 326 B.C., three years before Alexander's death. Before Alexander died at the age of thirty-two, he built a city on the Hydaspes that he called Bucephala in memory of his horse.

FROM CONTEMPORARY HISTORIANS.

THE PERFECT GOOD HORSE :

To have the Head and Legs of a Stag, the Ears and Tail of a Fox, the Neck of a Swan, the Breast of a Lyon, the Buttocks of a Woman, and the Feet of an Ass.

Attributed to GERVASE MARKHAM :
The Compleat Jockey, 17th Century.

I consider a horse to be sound which is perfect in structure,
and perfect in function

MR. MAVOR, LONDON VETERINARY SURGEON, *c.* 1800.

Fear thy God, speak evil of none,
Stick to the truth, and don't be done.

MRS. WILLIAM DAY.

THE PROPERTY OF AN OFFICER WHO IS GOING ABROAD

" Fifty—and five—sixty ; at sixty,
Sixty I'm bid ; sixty-one, sixty-two,
Sixty-two ; are you done ? Sixty-two,
Sixty-two " (the last moment you own him).
" Are all done ? I'm bid sixty-two.
The last time ! " And—rap ! " Sixty-two ! "
And you turn, sick at heart, as he trots to his stall,
Just to bid him farewell and go home, and—that's all.

. . . .

You bought him—remember ? One day in September,
Dog-poor and leg-weary and galled angry red,
He called to your heart with his pluck and his gallantry,
Captured your soul with the cock of his head.
And the pride that he carried, mixed up in a fair ;
And you couldn't go easily, leaving him there.
So you bought him and nursed him. He needed no schooling !
He knew it and loved it ; you knew by the fooling
He played when the season came round and you tried him ;
Remember that day ? What a glory to ride him !
Your youth and his knowledge, his courage, his power
(The best gifts to Man are the Horse and the Hour) ;
You trusted—he gave, and was glad in the giving ;
The world was a playground, and Life was worth living.

. . . .

It's India for you and a dealer for him,
And the yard as you leave it is damnably dim.

A. M. Harbord : *The Property of an Officer who is going abroad.*

For never man had friend
More enduring to the end,
Truer mate in every turn of time and tide.

LEARNING TO RIDE

TRAIN up a child in the way he should go, and when he is old he will not depart from it.

OLD PROVERB.

The first good steed his knees bestrode,
The first wild sound of songs that flowed
Through ears that thrilled and heart that glowed,
  Fulfilled his day with joy.

ALGERNON SWINBURNE.

An Old Irish huntsman's advice to the question put to him by the widow of his lord :—" Don't you think, Mick, it's time that Master Ulick learned to ride ? "

" My lady, get him a nice little horse, with some divil in him, of the chit-chat shape ; let him keep his legs to the pony's sides and his arms to his own. Tell him to keep his hands down and his heart and his head up ; and very soon, I go bail, he'll ride as well as the *Masther*, Heaven rest his soul ! "

For easy the lesson of the youthful train when instinct prompts, and example guides.

OLD PROVERB.

A perfect horseman knows neither fear nor anger.

Would you, a gentleman or lady see,
In as much elegance, as each would be,
Put them on horseback, and the science teach,
Of excellence in Horsemanship, to reach.
Why should so fine a picture be defac'd
By riding awkwardly, and not in taste ?

ANON.

He that will venture nothing must not get on horseback.

OLD SPANISH PROVERB.

The first mention in our history of the art of riding is in the tilts and tournaments which were practised in England for the first time in the reign of Stephen about the year 1140.

Knights, with a long retinue of their squires,
In gaudy liveries march and quaint attires;
One laced the helm, another held the lance,
A third the shining buckler did advance.
The courser paw'd the ground with restless feet,
And snorting foam'd and champ'd the golden bit.
The smiths and armourers on palfreys ride,
Files in their hand and hammers at their side;
And nails for loosen'd spears, and thongs for shields provide.
The yeomen guard the streets in seemly bands;
And clowns come crowding on, with cudgels in their hands.

Palamon and Arcite.

These tournaments were the prevailing entertainment of Christendom for many centuries, the French being particularly addicted to them, while the Gothic nations performed them in the depth of winter, on the ice. Amongst the principal requisites of knighthood was the accomplished management of the horse and the lance. Tournaments were held all over England, where traces can still be found of the spots on which they were held from the names of the surrounding places, the most famous being the Tilt-yard in St. James's Park. Smithfield was likewise famous for the frequent and splendid tournaments held there: adjoining it are Knightrider Street and Giltspur Street, the former so named, it is presumed, from the knights riding through it to the tournament at Smithfield, and the latter from the magnificent gilt spurs worn in those times being sold there.—P. B.

In his romance *Ivanhoe* Sir Walter Scott gives a description of a tournament or "passage of arms" held in the country:

Neither duty nor infirmity could keep youth or age from such exhibitions. The passage of arms, as it was called, which was to take place at Ashby, in the county of Leicester, as champions of the first renown were to take the field in the presence of Prince John himself, who was expected to grace the lists, had attracted universal attention, and an immense confluence of persons of all ranks hastened upon the appointed morning to the place of combat.

The scene was singularly romantic. On the verge of a wood, which approached to within a mile of the town of Ashby, was an extensive meadow of the finest and most beautiful green turf, surrounded on one side by the forest, and fringed on the other by some straggling oak trees, some of which had grown to an immense size. The ground, as if fashioned on purpose for the martial display which was intended, sloped gradually down on all sides to a level bottom, which was enclosed for the lists with strong palisades, forming a space of a quarter of a mile in length, and about half as broad. The form of the enclosure was an oblong square, save that the corners were considerably rounded off, in order to afford more convenience for the spectators. The openings for the entry of the combatants were at the northern and southern extremities of the lists, accessible by strong wooden gates, each wide enough to admit two horsemen riding abreast. At each of these portals were stationed two heralds, attended by six trumpets, as many pursuivants, and a strong body of men-at-arms, for maintaining order, and ascertaining the quality of the knights who proposed to engage in this martial game.

On a platform beyond the southern entrance, formed by a natural elevation of the ground, were pitched five magnificent pavilions, adorned with pennons of russet and black, the chosen colours of the five knights challengers. The cords of the tents were of the same colour. Before each pavilion was suspended the shield of the knight by whom it was occupied, and beside it stood his squire, quaintly disguised as a savage or silvan man, or in some other fantastic dress, according to the taste of his master and the character he was pleased to assume during the game. . . .

From the entrance into the lists a gently sloping passage, ten yards in breadth, led up to the platform on which the tents were pitched. It was strongly secured by a palisade on each side, as was the esplanade in front of the pavilions, and the whole was guarded by men-at-arms.

The northern access to the lists terminated in a similar entrance of thirty feet in breadth, at the extremity of which was a large enclosed space for such knights as might be disposed to enter the lists with the challengers, behind which were placed tents containing refreshments of every kind for their accommodation, with armourers, farriers, and other attendants, in readiness to give their services wherever they might be necessary.

The exterior of the lists was in part occupied by temporary galleries, spread with tapestry and carpets, and accommodated with cushions for the convenience of those ladies and nobles who were expected to attend the tournament. A narrow space betwixt these galleries and the lists gave accommodation for yeomanry and spectators of a better degree than the mere vulgar, and might be compared to the pit of a theatre. The promiscuous multitude arranged themselves upon large banks of turf prepared for the purpose, which, aided by the natural elevation of the ground, enabled them to overlook the galleries, and obtain a fair view into the lists. Besides the accommodation which these stations afforded, many hundreds had perched themselves on the branches of the trees which surrounded the meadow ; and even the steeple of a country church, at some distance, was crowded with spectators.

SIR WALTER SCOTT : *Ivanhoe.*

How easy is riding, after the first timidity is over, to supple and youthful limbs ! and there is no second fear. Oh, that ride ! That first ride ! most truly it was an epoch in my existence ; I still look back on it with feelings of longing and regret. People may talk of first love, but give me the flush, the triumph and the glorious sweat of a first ride, like mine on the mighty cob. My whole frame was shaken, it is true ; and during one long week I could hardly move foot or hand ; but what of that ? By that one trial I had become free, as I may say, of the whole equine species. No more fatigue, no more stiffness of joints after that first ride round the Devil's Hill on the cob. Oh, that cob ! That Irish cob !—May the sod lie lightly over the bones of the strongest, speediest, and most gallant of its kind ! Oh the days when, issuing from the barrack-gate of Templemore, we commenced our hurry-scurry just as inclination led, now across the fields, direct over stone walls and running brooks—mere pastime for the cob—sometimes along the road to Thurles and Holy Cross, even to distant Cahir ! What was the distance to the cob ?

It was thus that the passion for the equine race was first awakened within me, a passion which up to the present time has been rather on the increase than diminishing. It is no blind passion, the horse being a noble and generous creature, intended by the All-Wise to be the helper and friend of man, to whom he stands next in the order of creation. On many occasions of my life I have been much indebted to the horse, and found in him a friend and coadjutor, when human help and sympathy were not to be obtained. It is therefore natural enough that I should love the horse.

GEORGE BORROW : *The Autobiography of Lavengro*, 1851.

The undebased gipsy is a born horseman and horse jockey or coper. The word "jockey" is derived from a Romany word which means a whip.

SEAT

Some people tell you they ride by "balance" others by "grip." I think a man might as well say he played the fiddle by "finger," or by "ear." Surely in either case a combination of both is required to sustain the performance with harmony and success. The grip preserves the balance which in turn prevents the grip becoming irksome. To depend on the one alone is to come home very often with a dirty coat, to cling wholly by the other is to court as much fatigue in a day as ought to serve for a week. I have more than once compared riding to swimming, it seems to require the same buoyancy of spirits, the same venture of body, the same happy combination of confidence, strength, and skill.

The seat a man finds easiest to himself, says the inimitable Mr. Jorrocks, "will in all humane probability be the easiest to his 'oss!" and in this, as in every other remark of the humorous grocer, there is no little wisdom and truth. "If he go smooth, I *am*," (*J'y suis*) said a Frenchman, to whom a friend of mine offered a mount, "if he go rough, I shall not remain!" and doubtless the primary object of getting into a saddle is to stay there at our own convenience, so long as circumstances permit. But what a number of different attitudes do men adopt, in order to insure this permanent settlement. There is no position, from the tongs in the fender, to the tailor on his shop-board, into which the equestrian has not forced his unaccustomed limbs, to avoid involuntary separation from his beast. The dragoon of fifty years ago was drilled to ride with a straight leg, and his foot barely resting on the stirrup, whereas the oriental cavalry soldier, no mean proficient in the management of horse and weapon, tucks his knees up nearly to his chin, so that when he rises in the saddle he towers above his little Arab as if he were standing rather than sitting on its back. The position, he argues, gives him a longer reach, and stronger purchase for the use of sword and spear. If we are to judge by illuminated copies of Froissart, and other contemporary chronicles, it would seem that the armour-clad knight of the olden time, trusting in the depth and security of his saddle, *rode so long* so to derive no assistance whatever from his stirrups, sitting down on his horse as much as possible, in dread, maybe, lest the point of an adversary's lance should hoist him fairly out of his place over a cantle six inches high, and send him clanging to the ground, in mail

and plate, surcoat, helmet and plumes, with his lady-love, squires, yeomen, the marshals of the lists, and all his feudal enemies looking on !

. . . I dare say most of us can remember the mechanical horse exhibited in Piccadilly some ten or twelve years ago, a German invention, remarkable for its ingenuity and the wonderful accuracy with which it imitated, in an exaggerated degree, the kicks, plunges, and other outrages practised by the most restless of the species to unseat their riders. Shaped in the truest symmetry, clad in a real horse's skin, with flowing mane and tail, this automaton represented the live animal in every particular, but for the pivot on which it turned, a shaft entering the belly below its girths, and communicating through the floor with the machinery that set in motion and regulated its astonishing vagaries. On mounting, the illusion was complete. Its very neck was so constructed with hinges that on pulling at the bridle, it gave you its head without changing the direction of its body, exactly like an unbroken colt as yet intractable to the bit. At a word from the inventor, spoken in his own language to his assistant below, this artificial charger committed every kind of wickedness that could be devised by a fiend in equine shape. It reared straight on end ; it lunged forward with its nose between its forefeet, and its tail elevated to a perpendicular, awkward and ungainly as that of a swan *in reverse*. It lay down on its side ; it rose to its legs with a bounce, and finally, if the rider's strength and dexterity enabled him still to remain in the saddle, it wheeled round and round with a velocity that could not fail at last to shoot him out of his seat on to the floor, humanely spread with mattresses, in anticipation of this inevitable catastrophe. It is needless to say how such an exhibition drew, with so horse-loving a public as our own. No gentleman who fancied he could " ride a bit " was satisfied till he had taken his shilling's worth and the mechanical horse had put him on his back. But for the mattresses, Piccadilly would have counted more broken collar-bones than ever did Leicestershire in the blindest and deepest of its Novembers. Roughriders from the Life-Guards, Blues, Artillery, and half the cavalry regiments in the service, came to try conclusions with the spectre ; and, like antagonists of some automaton chess-player, retired defeated and dismayed.

But those who succeeded best, I remarked (and I speak with some little experience, having myself been indebted to the mattresses in my turn), were the horsemen who, allowing their loins to play freely, yielding more or less to every motion of the figure, did not trust exclusively for firmness of seat to the clasp of their knees and thighs. The mere balance rider had not a chance. The athlete who stuck on by main force found himself hurled into the air, with a violence proportioned to his own stubborn resistance ; but the artist who judiciously combined strength with skill, giving a little here that he might get a stronger purchase there, swaying his body loosely to meet and accompany every motion, while he kept his legs pressed hard against the saddle, withstood trick after trick, and shock after shock creditably enough, till a hint muttered in German that it was time to displace him, put such mechanism in motion as settled the matter forthwith. . . .

The shortest and surest way, however, of attaining a firm seat on horseback is, after all, to practise without stirrups on every available opportunity.

The late Captain Percy Williams, as brilliant a rider over a country as ever cheered a hound, and to whom few professional jockeys would have cared to give five pounds on a race-course, assured me that he attributed to the above self-denying exercise that strength in the saddle which used to serve him so well from the distance home. When quartered at Hounslow with his regiment, the 9th Lancers, like other gay young light dragoons, he liked to spend all his available time in London. There were no railroads in those days, and the coaches did not always suit for time ; but he owned a sound, speedy, high-trotting hack, and on this " bone setter " he travelled backwards and forwards twelve miles of the great Bath Road, with military regularity, half as many times a week. He made it a rule to cross the stirrups over his horse's shoulders the moment he was off the stones at either end, only to be replaced when he reached his destination. In three months' time, he told me, he had gained more practical knowledge of horsemanship, and more muscular power below the waist, than in all the hunting, larking, and riding-school drill of the previous three years.

Grace is, after all, but the result of repressed strength. The loose and easy seat that seems to sway so carelessly with every motion, can tighten itself by instinct to the compression of a vice, and the " prettiest rider," as they say in Ireland, is probably the one whom a kicker or back-jumper would find the most difficult to dislodge. No doubt in the field, the ride, the parade or the polo-ground a strong seat is the first of those many qualities that constitute good horsemanship. The real adept is not to be unseated by any catastrophe less conclusive than complete downfall of man and beast ; nay, even then he parts company without confusion, and it may be said of him as of " William of Deloraine," good at need in a like predicament :

" Still sate the warrior, saddle fast,
Till, stumbling in the mortal shock,
Down went the steed, the girthing broke,
Hurled in a heap lay man and horse."

But I have a strong idea Sir William did not let his bridle go even then.

G. J. Whyte Melville : *Riding Recollections.*

HANDS

Heavy hands make hard-mouthed horses.

His hand was like a chamois glove
And riding was his chief delight.

Though the Hand is to be firm and determined, to enforce a due submission and obedience, yet it must be soft, pliant, gentle and accommodating to the horse while he is united and cheerfully obedient while thereto. Hence the Hand must be sensible and discriminating whether the horse wishes to disengage himself from the restrictions of the Hand, or whether he wants a momentary liberty for his accommodation and ease. For instance, he will remove your hand if he wants to cough ; he will move his head if crampt by too long confinement, or to dislodge a fly, and the like. Now, the rider discovering the cause of such removal, will not correct (unless the horse, presuming on your complaisance, takes too much liberty) but rather allow a reasonable accommodation, and be light and pleasant while the horse is united and obedient.

If the Hand is held steady as the horse advances in the trot, the fingers will feel, by the contraction and dilation of the reins, a small sensation or tug, occasioned by the measure or cadence of every step. This sensation or tug, which is reciprocally felt in the horse's mouth, by means of the correspondence, is called the *appui* ; and while this *appui* is preserved between the Hand and mouth, the horse is in perfect obedience to the rider, the Hand directing him with the greatest ease so that the horse seems to work by the will of the rider, rather than the compulsion of the Hand.

Another excellence of the Hand is, a delicate susceptible feeling ; for some horses' mouths, when united to the extreme, as in *piaffs* and *pefades*, are so exquisitely light and delicate, that the *appui* would not break the finest hair ; the Hand, consequently, must possess the same exquisite degree of sensibility and delicacy.

I do not account him a good horseman, though he sit ever so firm on his horse, who has not, at least, a partial knowledge of the power and effects of the Hand. For no person can alter or improve his horse's mouth beyond the capacity of his own Hand. Hence, if your Hand is bad, you can never make your horse's mouth good ; and if your horse's mouth is good, you will soon reduce it to a level with your Hand.

JOHN ADAMS, RIDINGMASTER : *Analysis of Horsemanship*, 1799.

Remember he is as much your partner as any young lady entrusted to you in a ballroom.

G. J. Whyte Melville.

HANDS AND SEAT

The man who has good hands and seat—and they go very much together—is he who sits well down in the middle of his saddle in an easy natural position, the upper part of his body over his hips, or, if inclined either way, a little back; his thigh well down the flap of the saddle, and the lower part of his leg about covering the girth; the body supple, not resisting the motion of the horse. The elbows should always be under the shoulders, without stiffness, and the hands should give and take, so as not at any time to have a dull, hard feeling on the horse's mouth. The leg should work in unison with the hand. It will be found that the man who rides in the position described will, in applying the leg, draw it a little back, so that the horse feels the pressure just behind the girth. The man who has good hands and seat, will not, if the horse throws his head up and poke his nose out, immediately clutch the reins shorter and ram his legs or spurs into the animal's sides, but will drop his hand for a moment, and then, when the horse drops his nose, as he is almost certain to do, will quietly shorten his reins a little, and close the legs so as to endeavour to keep him there. . . .

Many more comparisons might be drawn between good and bad hands and seat, but perhaps these few are sufficient; and, to sum up, the best hands and seat are those in possession of the man with a good temper, between whom and his horse there is, so to speak, constant communication. He has always a feeling on his horse's mouth, but never holds on by it; he can tell by the feel of his horse if he contemplates doing anything out of the common, and can nearly always forestall him, without the horse seeming to be aware of it. He is always carried well and pleasantly. If his horse should by any means be startled and take a jump to one side or the other, he goes with him and does not pull his mouth about; in fact, it would appear that horse and man were one machine, possessed of one mind between them. If many people who keep horses—it would be too much to say who *ride* them—once got to understand how agreeable is the feeling of a horse going pleasantly and evenly into his bridle without pulling, at the same time feeling, as it were, every motion of the horse, they would never be satisfied with one that was not well broken, and would try to keep him up to the mark when once they really understood what riding meant.

Robert Weir: *Riding*, Badminton Library, 1891.

If the man's heart is in the right place, his horse will seldom fail him; and were we asked to name the one essential without which it is impossible to attain thorough proficiency in the saddle, we should not hesitate to say nerve.

Nerve, I repeat, in contradistinction to pluck. The latter takes us into a difficulty, the former brings us out of it. Both are comprised in the noble quality we call emphatically valour, but while the one is a brilliant and imposing costume, so is the other an honest wear-and-tear fabric, equally fit for all weathers, fine and foul.

"You shiver, Colonel—you are afraid," said an insubordinate Major, who ought to have been put under arrest then and there, to his commanding officer on the field of Prestonpans. "I *am* afraid, sir," answered the Colonel; "and if you were as much afraid as I am, *you would run away*!"

I have often thought this improbable anecdote exemplifies very clearly that most meritorious of all courage which asserts the domination of our will over our senses. The Colonel's answer proves he was full of valour. He had lots of pluck, but, as he was bold enough to admit, a deficiency of nerve. Now the field of Diana happily requires but a slight percentage of daring and resolution compared with the field of Mars. I heard the late Sir Francis Head, distinguished as a soldier, a statesman, an author, and a sportsman, put the matter in a few words, very tersely—and exceedingly to the point.

"Under fire," said he, "there is a guinea's-worth of danger, but it comes to you. In the hunting field, there is only three-ha'p'orth, but *you go to it*!"

In both cases, the courage required is a mere question of degree, and as in war, so in the chase, he is most likely to distinguish himself whose daring, not to be dismayed, is tempered with coolness, whose heart is always stout and hopeful, while he never loses his head. Now as I understand the terms pluck and nerve, I conceive the first to be a moral quality, the result of education, sentiment, self-respect, the second, a gift of nature, dependent on the health, the circulation, and the liver. As memory to imagination in the student, so is nerve to pluck in the horseman. Not the more brilliant quality, nor the more captivating, but sound, lasting, available for all emergencies, and sure to conquer in the long run. We will suppose two sportsmen are crossing a country equally well mounted, and each full of valour to the brim. A, to quote his admiring friends, "has the pluck of the devil!" B, to use a favourite expression of the saddle-room, "has a good nerve." Both are bound to come to grief over some forbidding rails at a corner, the only way out, in the line hounds are running, and neither has any more idea of declining than had poor Lord Strathmore on a similar occasion when Jem Mason halloaed to him, "Eternal misery on this side, my lord, and certain death on the other!" So they harden their hearts, sit down in their saddles, and this is what happens:

A's horse, injudiciously sent at the obstacle, *because* it is awkward, a turn too fast, slips in taking off, and strikes the top rail, which neither bends nor breaks, just below its knees. A flurried snatch at the bridle pulls its head in the air, and throws the animal skilfully to the ground at the moment it requires perfect freedom for a desperate effort to keep on its legs. Rider and horse roll over in an "imperial crowner," and rise to their feet looking wildly about them, totally disconnected, and five or six yards apart.

This is not encouraging for B, who is obliged to follow, inasmuch as the place only offers room for one at a time, but as soon as his leader is out of the way, he comes steadily and quietly at the leap. His horse, too, slips in the tracks of its fallen comrade, but as it is going in a more collected form, contrives to get its forelegs over the impediment, which catches it, however, inside the hocks, so that, balancing for a moment, it comes heavily on its nose. During these evolutions, B sits motionless in the saddle, giving the animal complete liberty of rein. An instinct of self-preservation and a good pair of shoulders turn the scale at the last moment, and though there is no denying "they had a squeak for it" in the scramble, B and his horse come off without a fall.

Now it was pluck that took both these riders into the difficulty, but nerve that extracted one of them without defeat.

G. J. WHYTE MELVILLE: *Riding Recollections.*

Xenophon, *c.* 430–355 B.C., a Greek writer, cavalry leader, and student of the horse and horsemanship, wrote the "Hippike," a treatise on horsemanship, as well as others on cavalry training and hunting, remarkable for their practical sense and humanitarian methods of breaking and riding. His maxims of so long ago have come down to us through the centuries and these first words on the art of horsemanship are as practical and up-to-date as the last modern words on equitation of to-day:—P. B.

An " imperial crowner."

But there is one rule to be inviolably observed above all others ; that is, never to approach the horse in a passion ; for anger never thinks of consequences, and forces us to do what we afterwards repent.

TRANSLATED FROM THE ORIGINAL GREEK : *Xenophon's Treatise on Horsemanship.*

So, to be masters of our horses, we must be masters of ourselves.

LIEUT.-COL. M. F. MCTAGGART : *Mount and Man*, 1925.

When a horse is shy of any thing, and will not come near it, he should be taught that there is no room for his apprehension. If this cannot be done otherwise, the rider should take hold of the thing which is the cause of this fright, should show it to him, and then endeavour gently to lead him up to it. On the contrary, if he should force him by blows and severity, they would enhance his terrors, and the horse would think that what he then suffers is absolutely occasioned by the thing of which he is afraid. He must take care not to offend or harass his mouth, by a rash and indiscreet hand.—*Xenophon.*

WHY DO HORSES SHY ?

The right way to deal with the problem is, firstly, to speak to him in a friendly and not boisterous way. The next thing is to apply a very strong pressure of the far side leg and rein so as to endeavour to keep the horse straight in the direction he should be going. We often see the reverse. We see the rider pulling the horse's head in towards the object. It is in circumstances such as these that the horse wants encouragement, not punishment, and the friendly guiding pressure of the man's legs to reassure him, and to help him.

MCTAGGART.

. . . and likewise, never to use the whip or spurs, but with great moderation and judgement.—*Xenophon.*

Everyone who rides does well to have a whip, stick, or crop in their hands, but it should seldom be used as a means of punishment.—MCTAGGART.

FAMOUS RIDERS

THEIR bones are dust, their spurs are rust,
Their souls are with the saints, we trust.
SIR WALTER SCOTT.

Like a swallow can Dick o'er the water-flood skim,
And Dick, like a duck, in the saddle can swim ;
Up the steep mountain-side like a cat he can crawl,
He can squeeze like a mouse through a hole in the wall !

He can tame the wild young one, inspirit the old,
The restive, the runaway, handle and hold ;
Sharp steel or soft-sawder, which e'er does the trick,
It makes little matter to hard-riding Dick.

Bid the chief from the desert bring hither his mare,
To ride on the plain against Dick if he dare ;
Bring Cossack or Mexican, Spaniard or Gaul,
There's a Dick in our village will ride round them all !

A whip is Dick's sceptre, a saddle Dick's throne,
And a horse is the kingdom he rules as his own ;
While grasping ambition encircles the earth,
The dominions of Dick are enclosed in a girth.

Three ribs hath he broken, two
But there hangs, it is said, ro
Still long odds are offer'd t
Will die, as he lived, in h

R. E. E

Dick Christian was born at Cot
and died 1862. That he was a wor
eleven falls off one horse in a day, he
rode all the most difficult horses in M
fresh ones in a week, besides schooling
only one fatal accident to his mount, c
which shot up into its chest.

EXTRACTS FROM DICK CHRISTIAN'S LECTURES :

This Marigold I must tell you about her—I have it all
see, Mr. Coke (William, nephew of the Earl of Leicester, a great

audacious men to ride he and Sir James Musgrave were to be sure !—he told me, I must always be with hounds—where they went, I must go, if it killed the horse ;—so this Marigold, I sent her at a hedge ;—when I was in the air, I sees my danger. Frightened ? God bless you ! I was never frightened in my life ; so I pulls her right back, just as she touched the bank, and shot her hind legs right under her ;—we made three landings of it ;—it was as steep as a house side ;—but you'll read all about it there ; and mind you bring the bit of print back.

DANGEROUS HUNTING EXPLOIT :

The following extraordinary feat was last week inadvertently performed by the celebrated rider and rough veteran, Dick Christian, of Melton Mowbray. He was mounted on Mr. Coke's chestnut mare Marigold, and out with the Quorn hounds near Holwell mouth, when he charged a thick cut hedge 4½ feet high, which he cleared in good style, the mare alighting on a bank about a yard wide, with all her four feet together ; immediately below this bank is a steep declivity into an old quarry or stone pit called Sot's Hole, about 12 yards deep ; the failure of the bank where friend Dick had thus suddenly deposited his whole capital, must have [illegible]ved fatal : luckily it stood firm, and the generous
[illegible] nded boldly forward, reaching the bottom
[illegible] nt of which we subjoin—to the amaze-
[illegible] hers who witnessed this unprecedented
[illegible] ll fixed in his saddle when the gallant
[illegible] steed and rider were perfectly un-
[illegible] nd wondered for the moment what
[illegible] praise cannot be given to our hardy
[illegible] ve, his firm and vigorous hand, and
[illegible] ir. The following is a correct state-
[illegible] e ledge not being included :—Over
[illegible] in a right line ; second leap, 10′ 6″ ;
[illegible] ′ 3″. . . .

[illegible] t one day, when we found at Cream Gorse.
[illegible] th's young horses, and he dropped in the ditch
[illegible] ullfinch : he jumped high enough, but he didn't spread
[illegible] grey he bought of Bill Wright, of Sysonby. He must have
[illegible] on me if I had pulled him ; so I slips off, and let him go, and he

ran to Brooksby with them. The whole field, 150 on 'em were behind me: and I snuggled in against the side of the hedge and over they goes. I could see the shoes, 600 on 'em, glittering right above and beside me, and not one of them made a mistake; they'd have killed me if they had. I wasn't frightened—not I. Just as each of 'em passed over my head, I gives a bit of a shout and a chuckle to 'em for encouragement like. They were all at me next day. First one comes up, and then another, and says "What the devil, Dick, did you keep hollering at us for, yesterday, at that fence? We heard you, but we couldn't see you." "You'd have made a noise too," I told 'em, "to see you gentlemen come over me like that." . . .

The biggest fence I ever took was on one of Sir James Musgraves' 400 guinea gentlemen; he gave Sir James such a purl near Shangton Holt—turned right over with him. I got off and went to him but he says, "You go on, Dick." I looks round, and see him fall down again; so I went back, and I says, "Sir James, I shan't leave you." He was laid up a good six weeks, and he sends for me. "You must ride that horse of mine, Dick: If you kill him I shan't blame you; but if you stop at anything, you shall ride for me no more. I shall send people to keep their eye on you." "Well," says I, "Sir James, if you are not afraid of your horse, I'm not afraid of my neck." We met at the Punch Bowl, and I knew there were two or three to look out; and blame me, I did ride just! One field from Dalby, my word! I did send him with some powder at a bullfinch. I thought the horse was a long time in the air. They measured the jump, nearest foot from taking off to nearest foot on landing, right through the hedge; and what d'ye think it was? Thirty-five and a half feet! It's truth, I'll warrant it: there are gentlemen living who know it. . . .

(Later Mr. Tilbury's Culverthorpe jumped 37 feet over hurdles at Newport-Pagnell; and in a steeplechase at Leamington, near Warwick, in 1847 Captain Little's Chandler cleared 39 feet over the brook in which several horses and their riders were scrambling at the time. This jump remains the record long-jump for a horse in this country.)—P. B.

Grimaldi, he was a charming horse; he never would look at water first. Mr. Osbaldeston he comes to me in Day's shop here and he says, "I want you, Dick, to go to Brixworth directly: I've made a match with Colonel Charritie's Napoleon for 500 guineas, over the Dunchurch country: there's a brook, and Grimaldi's lost me two races already that way." So I said I'd like to go to Croxton races, and I'd be at Brixworth at two in the morning; and so I was there, sure enough, and got him over some water the first time, after he had smelt at it a bit, and made him quite handy. The Squire and me, we went over the ground, and the Squire, he says, "Grimaldi will never jump this water, Dick." I says, "I'll bet you a guinea he will, Squire." I went and fathomed it, and found a place; so I told him: "When you're running I'll stand there, and put me hat on the top of my whip; come right to me, and keep him going." Bless you! he jumped it like nothing at all, and won. Becher was on Napoleon; he was stronger, I think, than Oliver; Jem Mason's not so hard as them two. The Clown that won here the other day, reminded me for all the world of Vyvyan when he was coming to the brook. Vyvyan was quite as big, a great slamming horse; no trouble to ride; he went sailing along in a snaffle, and Becher just niggling at him a bit. I rode against him and Becher at Dunchurch, and gave them such a tying up. Lord Waterford (Harry Beresford, 3rd ("Mad") Marquis, 1811–1859. Broke his neck) and Lord Macdonald (Godfrey, 4th Baronet 1809–1863) were in that race. I was on Warwick, one of Sir Edward Mostyn (7th Baronet 1785–1841 of Talacre). They laid 20–1 against me. He was a little horse, very hot; my eyes, such a jumper! I didn't keep long with them, but took a line for myself. Vyvyan got first round to the flag, and then the Marquis (of Waterford) and then I, the Marquis was going wide, and shouts I, "My lord, where *are* you going to?" I slipped right up to Vyvyan, and hang me if I'd leave him; didn't Becher just go on at me! Every fence it was, "Dick, you'll be on top of me; pray Dick, do keep off." That was it all the way back; I wouldn't have it; I says, "This is my line, and here I'll stick"; and I did too. I'd got my horse as fast as wax, and I thought win I must. We were in the air together over the last fence; then Becher he sets at his horse, and he just shoves his head afore me. "Now," I says, "I'll see what I've got," and blame me if my horse didn't stop dead as if he was shot. I called to them to turn his head to the wind, or he would be down. I never got him past the post; he went backwards, he was so beat; he never got above two miles before or since that day; he was a bad-hearted one, but very brilliant; that's as nice a ride as ever I had; how he did jump, to be sure! when Becher got back to the weighing tent he spoke up, "Gentlemen, if I had Christian's nerve, I'd give all I had in the world." I've had lots of accidents: I've had my shoulder out, this here leg broke, and two of my ribs; I never broke my collar bone, I am so precious thick set there, and they can't get at it. Horses, bless you! I've known 'em get out of a ditch, and put their fore-feet on each of my shoulders ; my coat's been all split up by them. I broke two ribs from a dog-cart when I was 76. . . .

I once jumped a whole flock of sheep near Gadesby, in Mr. Osbaldeston's time. I think we'd found at the Coplow. They had scruddled into a corner, just like that near those pens. The hounds were running like mad. I was leading. I sent my horse at the rails, and clears the sheep, every one of 'em. My horse he hits the top of the rail, and goes clean bang on to his head. The shepherd, he shouts, "*Now hang you, that just serves you right.*" I says, "So it does, old fellow," and I gathers myself up, and goes on, and we kills the fox at Ragdale.

THE DRUID : *Silk and Scarlet, Post and Paddock.*

SQUIRE OSBALDESTON

Come, I'll show you a country that none can surpass,
For a flyer to cross like a bird on the wing,
We have acres of woodland and oceans of grass,
We have game in the autumn and cubs in the spring.
We have scores of good fellows hang out in the shire,
But the best of them all is the Galloping Squire.

The Galloping Squire to the saddle has got,
While the dewdrop is melting in gems on the thorn
From the kennel he's drafted the pick of his lot,
How they swarm to his cheer ! How they fly to his horn !
Like harriers turning or chasing like fire,
"I can trust 'em, each hound !" says the Galloping Squire.

One wave of his arm to the covert they throng,
"Yoi ! wind him ! and rouse him ! By Jove ! he's away !"
Through a gap in the oaks see them speeding along,
O'er the open like pigeons, "They *mean* it to-day !"
You may jump till you're sick—you may spur till you tire !
"For it's catch 'em who can !" says the Galloping Squire.

G. J. WHYTE MELVILLE : *The Galloping Squire.*

George Osbaldeston was born in 1786, his first pack of hounds were Southern hounds with which he hunted hare. At the age of twenty-one, he had a pack of dwarf foxhounds, followed by the Burton, bought from Lord Monson, 1810–1813, Lord Harrington's in 1814, then the Derbyshire and Atherstone countries 1815–1817. In this year he bought the Quorn from Assheton Smith which he hunted for ten seasons, except for a brief interruption owing to illness. Finally the Pytchley 1827–1834. He died in 1866.

The outstanding athlete of his day. Cricketer, game shot, billiards player, and prize fight referee, as well as a horseman, jockey, and breeder of foxhounds. The Squire was a born gambler, he would bet on anything, one had only to tell him that he could not do this, or that, for him to reply immediately "I'll bet you I could." A man of tremendous physical strength and courage, yet lacking in moral courage, kindhearted to a degree he fell an easy prey to unscrupulous agents, sharpers, and crooks of all kinds. "Squire of England," "The Little Wonder," "Little Ossey," "The Moonlight Hunter," and "The Hercules of Horsemen" were some of the nicknames given to him, in admiration and friendship by those who knew him.—P. B.

OSBALDESTON'S MATCHES

Here I may relate the story of my own steeplechase matches; I rode six and won them all. . . . We matched Grimaldi a second time; this race (6 April 1833) was against the grey horse belonging to General Charritie which I mentioned before, giving him two stone. The line was in the Dunchurch country, and nearly up to Dunchurch, the distance five miles. I rode Grimaldi and Captain Becher the General's horse. There was a good brook about a mile from the winning post and this was so swollen by the heavy rains it was like a small river. Grimaldi was not fond of water, but I sent him so fast that he was obliged to jump at it. He jumped as far as he could, but the brook was too wide for him and we went in, overhead. It was with difficulty we got out. I was of course soaked, and my boots were full of water; also the horse was so frightened that I could not mount for a few minutes. The consequence was that Becher, who had cleared the brook, was nearly three fields ahead of me. However, when Grimaldi did suffer me to mount, his superior speed enabled us to catch him, but only when we were within fifty yards of the end. Nevertheless, I won easily.

The sixth and last steeplechase match I rode was made under the following circumstances: Captain Becher was very sore at his defeat on General Charritie's grey, and after that match was continually singing the praises of

Clinker. I had a bay horse I called Clasher, which I bought of a farmer in Lord Yarborough's country; whether he was thoroughbred I don't know, but he had all the appearance of it. He was an extraordinary fencer, a capital water-jumper, and very fast. One day after dinner Becher was vaunting the merits of Clinker, and I said I would match him with Clasher. He laughed, evidently thinking I meant it as a joke; but finding I was in earnest he came to terms and the match was made. I stipulated that if Clasher should be lame it was void. . . . It was inserted in the Articles that we were both to go over the line before starting. This we did the day before the match with the late Sir Harry Goodricke, who was my umpire, and Captain White, who was Ross's. There were two brooks, one of which was wide, the other a mere nothing. Somebody remarking that the former was a pretty big jump, Goodricke made light of it, saying that he could do it on the horse he was riding. He rode at the brook three or four times, but his horse would not look at it. As I knew the line thoroughly I agreed with my head groom that I should make the running. We started near Dalby on the Melton side and finished within a quarter of a mile of Tilton-on-the-Hill, one of the finest lines in Leicestershire, and very severe, being hilly, high-ridged furrow, and deep. I forgot to mention that Dick Christian, one of the best riders of that day, rode Clinker. About half-way was Sir Harry's brook, and in the same field was a haystack, and the best place to take the brook was to leave the stack on the left hand. While going up a strong hill in the same field, before reaching the haystack, Christian said, "I beat you, for a hundred!" Turning my head, I saw him bearing to the other end of the field and shouted, "Where are you riding to? This is the line!" At the same time I saw a man on horseback close to the brook. I afterwards discovered that there was a ford which they had found the day before, but I knew nothing about it. Christian walked Clinker through it, and lost the race by doing so. My horse cleared the water with about a yard to spare. The next field was a large one and hilly, and covered with mole-hills. There was a sheep-track in the direct line, and I made all sail along it. Christian lost about 60 yards through walking through the brook, and having to gallop uphill, over the molehills. He nearly caught me at the end of the field, but I knew he must have distressed his horse, and made as strong running as I could down to the next brook. We had then to rise another hilly field which was within two of the winning post. There was a baulk, as they call it, along a hedgeside, and through this hedge was an opening which was the only practicable way out of the field. It was so intricate that we had agreed to place a man opposite to it, and the moment the fellow saw I was in front he hid himself in the ditch. I saw him under my feet, for luckily I determined to go at the first opening I saw, and it happened to be the right one. At this moment Christian's horse's nose nearly touched the tail of mine. We had to turn short to the left and jump a moderate fence into the winning field, and went at it almost abreast. His horse was so dreadfully distressed that he tumbled into it, and I cantered on to the winning chair. My horse was much distressed also ; so much so that I thought at the time, if I can clear this fence I shall win, because the ground Christian had lost, going wide of that ford and crossing the molehill field, besides the pace I had ridden, must have beaten him.

Squire Osbaldeston, His Autobiography : Edited by E. J. Cumming.

Dick Christian in his Lecture in *Post and Paddock* gives this account of the famous match : Clinker's and Clasher's was a great match : they said it was 1500 guineas a side. They sent for me the night before, did Captain White and Captain Ross, and locked me into their room : then they gave me their orders ; they says, " We mean you to wait, Dick," I said, " You'd better let me let the horse go along, gentlemen, and not upset him ; he'll take a deal more out of himself by waiting." So I got them persuaded round. Old Driver the groom was outside, and he comes up to me—" What do they shay ? What do you want to wait for ? " So I told him I was to go along, and that pleased him, it did. We thought it was all right then. We weighed at Dalby, the Squire and I—bless me ! I never was in such condition—and away we trotted to Gartree Hill. They were walking the horses about, and Captain Ross, he says to me, " Clinker looks well." " He looks too well, Captain," I said. Then he lifted me up, and he tells me the orders were changed, and I must wait. " It's giving away a certainty," says I, " and if I get a fall then I am all behind." But it was no manner of use talking. Sir Vincent Cotton and Mr. Gilmour they started us, and Mr. Maher he was umpire. We rode twelve stone apiece ; I was in tartan, and the Squire, of course he'd be in green. When we were at the post, he says, " Now, Christian, I know what your orders are. I do ask one thing ; don't jump on me if I fall." * I said, " I'll give you my word, Squire, I won't." The gentlemen, they could hardly keep with us, and some of them had two or three horses fixed. We were almost touching each other over Sharplands, and just before the road I says, " Squire, you're beat for a £100," but he never made no answer. Joe Tomlin and Charles Christian (Dick's brother) they stood close against Twyford Brook : I got well over that. Then we had some rails—such stiff uns ! Clasher hits them with all four legs, and chucked the Squire right on to his

* The Squire had been jumped on in the hunting field and his leg badly broken. He was always afterwards nervous of anyone riding in his pocket.—P. B.

neck ; Clinker took 'em like a bird. We were each in a mess then ; the Squire, he lands in a bog, and his horse makes a dead stop ; it did take a deal out of him ; then I jumps right into a dung heap, up to Clinker's knees ; we had no manner of idea the things was there. Going up John o' Gaunt's field we were together, but I turns to get some rails in the corner ; he was such a good one at rails, was Clinker ; I thought he was winning, but, deary me, down he comes at the last fence. Clinker he lays for some minutes, and then he gets up as lively as ever ; the horse looked in no manner of form, as round as a hoop, for all the world as if he was going to Horncastle Fair. They held Clasher up, and they flung water in his face, and he won in the last hundred yards from superior training, and that's the honest truth. Many didn't like Clinker but I never got on so good a steeplechaser. I'll tell you though one that was better, that's Coningham ; I won the Grantham Steeplechase on him, and Mr. Greene bought him for 200 gns. How hard "The Squire" did ride that match to be sure ! I went up to call on him one afternoon at St. John's Wood, and he pointed to that picture of the finish, hanging up just opposite the fireplace, and he says to me : "Dick, that Clasher and Clinker day beat me a deal more than the two hundred miles."

THE DRUID : *Post and Paddock*, 1856

THOMAS ASSHETON SMITH

But I thought, "I'd give something to have his receipt,
This rum one to follow, this bad one to beat."

ADAM LINDSAY GORDON.

He was born in London in 1776. Master of the Quorn 1806–1816, the Burton 1816–1824. For two seasons he gave up mastership while he hunted at Belvoir and in the neighbouring counties. In 1826 he moved to Penton Lodge, Andover, where he created a new hunting country. On the death of his father in 1828, he came into the family estate at Tedworth, and proceeded to hunt the unhunted Tedworth country with his own hounds for thirty-two seasons, during which time no subscriptions of any sort were ever asked for. He died in 1859. The number of foxes he killed during his mastership of hounds is indicated by his remark to a fellow sportsman : he had cut off fifteen hundred brushes with a pocket knife which he afterwards lost in West Woods. Early in life he hunted regularly with Lord Sefton, who succeeded the famous Meynell in Leicestershire. Lord Sefton's huntsman was Stephen Goodall, who, though an excellent sportsman, was incapacitated by his weight from living with his hounds when running hard. "I always like, Mr. Tom Smith," said Goodall to him, "to see you out on a *grey* horse, for then I know where the hounds are, and the shortest way to get to them : and am satisfied, when *you* are with them, *I* shall not be missed." In the famous Billesdon Coplow run, when only twenty-four years old, Mr. Smith was allowed to have the best of it down to the brook at Enderby, where his horse fell in. He told a friend that he bought the horse he that day rode, called Furze-cutter, for £26, and sold him after the run to Lord Clonbrock for £400 ; "A pretty good comment," he remarked, "on the place I maintained that day."—P. B.

The following anecdote is related by a Mr. Davy, whose prowess has been recorded by Nimrod, and of whom Mr. Smith said, "He was the only man of whose riding I was ever jealous."

A large field was assembled at Ashby Pastures, and a fox went away with the pack close at his brush. A long green drive ran parallel with the fields, down which all the horsemen rode save *one*. A high blackthorn hedge screened the hounds from their view, and they were riding for hard life. All at once some horse was heard on the same side as the hounds, rattling over the gates, and crashing through the bullfinches at such a pace, that Davy and another remarked, "Some fellow's horse purled him and run away." The illusion however was dispelled by the hounds swinging across the drive, and Tom Smith, on Jack-o'-Lantern, sailing by their side ; having beaten every man among them, though they had only to gallop over plain grass, while he had to encounter both gates and fences, and of the stiffest character. This, Davy confessed, was one of the greatest triumphs in horsemanship he had ever witnessed.

The history of the education of Jack-o'-Lantern was thus related by Tom Edge, an intimate friend of the Squire, and for many years his messmate at Quorn :

We were riding to covert through a line of bridle gates, when we came to a new double oaken post and rail fence. "This is just the place to make my colt a good timber jumper," said the Squire, "so you shut the gate, and ride away fast from the fence." This was accordingly done, when the Squire rode at the rails, which Jack taking with his breast, gave both himself and his rider such a fall that their respective heads were looking towards the fence they had ridden at. Up rose both at the same time, as if nothing very particular had happened. "Now," said Tom Smith, "this will be the making of the horse ; just do as you did before, and ride away." Edge did so, and Jack flew the rails without touching, and was a first-rate timber fencer from that day. What made the feat the more remarkable was, that it did not come off in a run, but in what is called " cold blood " !

Jack-o'-Lantern was a particularly quiet and good-tempered horse. When Mr. Lindow had broken his collar-bone, and was quite unable to hold the Clipper even with the " clipper-bit," Mr. Smith changed horses with him for the day. The meet was at Scoling's Gorse, near Melton. Mr. Lindow rode Jack with one arm in a sling, and the Clipper was brought out with bit-checks, some eight inches long, and the huge attendant curb-chain. Everyone thought Mr. Smith bewitched, because he would not mount until the curb-chain was taken off, and after pledging themselves that he would never be able to pull him up till he reached the sea coast, they heard early in the afternoon that " Mr. Smith had run away with the Clipper, and that he could never go fast enough for him any one part of the way. . . ."

Mr. Smith once took a most extraordinary leap in Lincolnshire. The hounds came to a cut or navigable canal, called the Fosdyke, over which there were two bridges, one a bridle bridge, the other used for carts. (They cross the canal into the lands of different land-owners, which accounts for their proximity.) At one end of these bridges there is usually a high gate leading into the field adjoining the canal, and along each side there is a low rail to protect persons going over. Smith rode along one of these bridges, and found the gate at the end locked, whereupon seeing the gate open at the end of the parallel bridge, he immediately put his horse at the rails, and jumped across and over the opposite rails, on to the other bridge, to the surprise and gratification of all who witnessed the feat.

It is well known what a number of brooks there are in the Quorn and Belvoir countries, and most sportsmen, if they were never out with Mr. Smith, have at all events heard what a capital hand he was at getting over them. He once charged the river Welland, which divides the counties of Leicester, Northampton, and Rutland, and is said to be altogether impracticable, at the end of one of the most desperate runs ever known. This knack he had of getting across water is to be attributed to his resolute way of riding to hounds, by which his horses knew that it was in vain to refuse whatever he might put them at. A remarkable example of this occurred in the Harborough country. He was galloping at three-parts speed down one of the larger grass fields which abound in that district, in the act of bringing his hounds to a scent, and was looking back to see if they were coming. Exactly in the middle of the field and in the line immediately before his horse, was a pool of water, into which the animal leaped, thinking it useless to refuse, and of course unaware that he was not expected to take it. This horse would doubtless have jumped into the Thames or the Severn in a similar manner, had they been before him. . . . His wonderful influence over his hunters was strongly exemplified at another time, but in rather a different manner. He had mounted, on his celebrated horse Cicero, a friend who complained of having nothing to ride :

> " A sportsman so keen, that he rides miles to covert,
> To look at a fence, he dares not ride over."

The hounds were running breast high across the big pasture-lands of Leicestershire, and Cicero was carrying his rider like a bird, when a strong flight of rails had almost too ugly an aspect of height, strength, and newness, for the liking of our friend on his " mount." The keen eye of Assheton Smith, as he rode beside him, at once discerned that he had no relish for the timber, and seeing that he was likely to make the horse refuse, he cried out, "Come up, Cicero ! " His well-known voice had at once the desired effect, but Cicero's rider, by whom the performance was not intended, left his " seat " vacant, fortunately without any other result than a roll upon the grass. . . .

Among Mr. Smith's sporting congregation were not a few of the clergy, and these were never far in the rear of the Squire. He was once entering the house of a certain divine, where his hounds met that morning, accompanied by the late Lord George Bentinck. " What profession is this gentleman of ? " asked his Lordship, as they entered the drawing-room. " A parson," replied the Squire, and pointing to the pictures of eminent sportsmen which adorned the walls, added, " Don't you see the portraits of his favourite bishops ? . . ."

The riding of Dick Knight, huntsman to the Pytchley at the time Mr. Smith led the Quorn, was of a character very similar to that of our Squire. An annual visitor to Northamptonshire was in the habit of riding so close to Dick as he could, but was invariably beaten in a run. At the commencement of the season, the gentleman was on a new horse, a clipper. He said to Knight, " You won't beat me to-day, Dick ! " " Won't I, sir," was the reply. " If you do, I'll give you the horse," said the gentleman. The one rode for the horse, the other for his honour. At last they came to an unjumpable place, which could only be crossed by going between the twin stems of a tree, barely wide enough to admit a horse. At it went Dick, throwing his legs across his horse's withers, and got *through*. The horse was sent to him next morning. . . .

E. EARDLEY-WILMOT: *A Famous Foxhunter,* Reminiscences of the late Thomas Assheton Smith.

"Nimrod" says in his *Hunting Reminiscences*:

I have a long list in letter S, in my alphabetical catalogue of eminent riders, and of course lots of Smiths, and there can be no hesitation as to the best claim to number one, namely, T. Assheton Smith, Esq., of Tedworth House, Hants, late owner of, and huntsman to, the Quorn hounds, and at present (1841) hunting a very good pack of his own in Hampshire. Now I am not going to give merely my own opinion of Mr. Thomas Assheton Smith, as a horseman, a rider to hounds, but shall lay before my readers that of all the sporting world, at least all who have seen him in the field; which is, that taking him from the first day's hunting of the season to the last, place him on the best horse in his stable or the worst, he is sure to be with his hounds, and *close to them too.* In fact, he has undoubtedly proved himself the best and hardest rider England ever saw, and it would be vain in any man to dispute his title to that character. But we might as well attempt to make a blind man an optician, a lame man a dancing-master, or a one-armed man a fiddler, as to suppose that any gentleman could arrive at this ultra state of perfection in a very difficult art, which horsemanship undoubtedly is, unless nature had been prodigal of the requisites. Setting aside the daring, undaunted, not-to-be-denied determination of Mr. Smith to get to hounds, despite of any and all difficulties which may have opposed him, the result of strongly braced nerves and great physical powers,—let us look at him in his saddle. Does he not look like a workman? Observe how lightly he sits! No one would suppose him to be a twelve-stone man. And what a firm hand he has on his horses! How well he puts them at their fences, and what chances he gives them to extricate themselves from any scrape they may have gotten into. He never hurries them then; no man ever saw Tom Smith ride fast at his fences, at least at large ones (brooks excepted), let the pace be what it may; and what a treat it is to see him jump water! His falls, to be sure, have been innumerable; but what very hard-riding man does not get falls? Hundreds of Mr. Smith's falls may be accounted for: he has measured his horse's pluck by his own, and ridden at hundreds of non-feasible places, with the chance of getting over them somehow. Bravo!

The mightiest hunter that ever " rode across Belvoir's sweet vale."

Mr. Smith, you must be number *one* for, by Heavens ! there will never be such another Mr. Smith as long as the world stands. . . .

" Dorset " writing in the *Sporting Magazine*, November 1836, says :

Of Mr. Smith, as a huntsman, it is needless to speak here, or indeed, anywhere. He ranks with the first professors of this noble science ; and as the *first horseman of the age*, as well as the most *accomplished huntsman* of the present day, his name will be enrolled historically in the deathless pages of the chronicles of the chase, and among those who have advanced and aided the political economy of his country in one of its most important departments. . . .

Mr. Smith was the originator of the gun-boats now generally introduced into the English and French navies. . . . Little perhaps did the spectators, who proudly gazed not long since upon the goodly swarm of those dark hulls at Spithead, know that the projector of them was a foxhunter, and that to a foxhunter's clear head and far-seeing eye was the gallant Wildman mainly indebted for the " single little vessel " (the *Staunch*) with which he demolished four large junks in the Chinese seas. . . .

And " The Druid " :

He was the mightiest hunter that ever " rode across Belvoir's sweet vale " or wore a horn at his saddle bow.

" Scrutator " in *Baily's Magazine*, 1861, describes Thomas Assheton Smith and " Squire " Osbaldeston as :

The two most brilliant stars which have ever arisen in our hunting hemisphere ; in whom every requisite was combined—genius and talents of the highest order—energy and activity—quickness of decision—coolness in action.

COUNT MORITZ SANDOR (1805–1878)

Was a Hungarian aristocrat and like our Squire Jack Mytton performed the most incredible and dangerous feats of horsemanship merely for the fun and devil of frightening and amazing his companions. It is said that Count Sandor learnt to ride before he could walk. At the age of sixteen his feats had caused him to be nicknamed "The Horseman of Hell." His exploits became legendary, and his pranks more and more dangerous as he flirted with death. The fact that he broke legs and arms made not the slightest difference to his unbounded confidence in himself and his mounts. He once tried to jump the ship bridge at Pressburg but fell heavily; although badly cut and bleeding he remounted and cleared the barrier at the second attempt. At the fair at Heiligenkreuz, Vienna, he jumped over a pot-maker's booth on his horse Pyrrhus. The owner of the booth had purposely piled his pots high, in the hope that some of them would be knocked over and broken, and so paid for, but the Count cleared the lot, to the accompaniment of the pot-maker's curses. One evening he rode up to the second storey of the White Swan Inn. Visiting his brother-in-law, Count Kegelvich, in Pest, he rode his horse Tartar up the stairs and along a narrow balcony. He found that the Count was out and the door locked. He therefore had to go back the way he had come; the balcony was only three feet wide and, as it was winter, covered with ice. The horse he was riding was afraid to go backwards and showed an inclination to rear up and jump down into the courtyard below. As he reared Count Sandor swung him round so that he landed again facing in the opposite direction. At Pistjan on the River Waag, he jumped from the bank into the ferry-boat which had already left the bank. In Pistjan also he played billiards on horseback. In 1842 he won a race against a locomotive for a wager. In the wood at Raro he hunted a stag, chasing it round and round between the trees until it dropped from exhaustion. In the Prater, Vienna, he escaped from a boring Baron by jumping over a cart laden with a thick oak-tree trunk, inviting the Baron to follow him. Also in the Prater, he made three cabs stand wheel to wheel, then removed the middle one. From a distance of 200 yards he galloped his six-in-hand (four abreast leading and a pair behind) between the two remaining cabs. The two outside horses had to squeeze together to get through, but nothing was touched. After this episode he was forbidden to drive with a six-in-hand, as that was the privilege of the King. Count Sandor replied in writing that anyone had the right to drive with as many horses as he liked, provided that he did not harness them in pairs, one pair in front of the other. To deliver this note he drove his six-in-hand at the gallop into the police headquarters at Vienna. When his 74-year-old gardener was dying, Sandor went to see him. On his favourite horse he jumped in through the window, so frightening the dying man that he was back at work, fully recovered, within two days. On the bridge at Raat the watch attempted to halt Sandor for riding too fast and dangerously, but he jumped over their crossed bayonets, bidding them a gay " good-night " as he rode away. In Buda he jumped clean over four outstretched swords held at shoulder height by four officers. During a steeplechase at Pardubitz, on his mare, Red Rose, he jumped a swollen stream, clearing 31 feet 3 inches. In the course of his career Count Sandor broke most of the bones in his body, and it is recorded that he put his knee out of joint no fewer than twenty-seven times. The luckiest escape of his career was when his horse, Gonos, shied and leapt over the brink of a 30-foot quarry at Bia. The Count fainted. The horse landed between broken rocks and a stone wall, on the only possible spot where he would suffer no damage. Both escaped unhurt with the Count still in the saddle. In 1850 his exploits came to an end when he was seized with madness, becoming a helpless wreck until he died twenty-eight years later. Even his funeral was not without incident. The six horses that drew his coffin in the funeral procession ran away. Racing through Banja they finally crashed into the cemetery, coming to a stop among the graves, just in front of the Sandor family tomb.

Notes from LEO SINGER : *Riding,* June 1939.

Count Sandor, he was an odd un, he was ; he said " He did come to von little place, called Meltone." Then they sent him to the tailor as lived at South Croxton, to get his breeches made ; it was on a Sunday too after Church ; but off he would go. When he comes back, he said, " When I did leave the town I did come to a door ; de horse he would not open de door, so I make him jump over de door, and as I come back, I did jump all de doors."

THE DRUID : " Dick Christian's Lecture," *Post and Paddock,* 1856.

FREDERICK ARCHER

> Genius is one per cent. inspiration and ninety-nine per cent. perspiration.

But those head finishes ! When the finest horseman in the world had a mount worthy of his genius—for he had genius ! When every inch was disputed by jockeys who were his equals in many respects, when a mass of bright silk, white breeches, and glossy thoroughbreds rounded Tattenham Corner " all of a heap," and Archer, hugging the white rails from start to finish as was his wont, suddenly shot out of the Derby group, amidst yells for the favourite, which lasted until the numbers went up and the " all right " was called. Oh! those days when racing was the finest of the fine arts; long will they be remembered, never will they be seen again, for Archer is dead.

Badminton Magazine, 1897.

Frederick James Archer was born at Cheltenham in 1857. His father was a noted steeplechase jockey who rode Little Charley to win the Grand National in 1858, and his mother Emma Hayward, a tall, dark aristocratic-looking girl, was the daughter of William Hayward, the highly respected landlord of the King's Arms at Prestbury. From his earliest days Archer was brought up to be a jockey. When only eleven years old he won a steeplechase at Bangor on a noted pony, Maid of Trent, and two years later, 1870, he won a Nursery at Chesterfield on Athol Daisy. In 1872 he won the Cesarewitch on Salvanos, and the Two Thousand Guineas on Atlantic in 1874. From that day his name was made. The effect of his young wife's premature death on Archer's impulsive, passionate, and highly strung nature, together with perpetual wasting, brought on fits of melancholy and finally, while ill with typhoid fever in 1886, he shot himself with a revolver. Archer had 8084 mounts in England and rode 2748 winners, including five Derbys, four Oaks, and the St. Leger six times. Lord Falmouth had first claim on Archer's services and the nickname of " The Tinman " originated from the mines on his patron's Cornish estate, although another source claims that the nick-name arose on account of the jockey being saving with his money. He was careful, it is true, but he could be very generous especially to brother jockeys down on their luck, and he often gave away a fiver in a quiet sort of way.

Archer's success apart from his brilliant ability was due to his determination to win. He would sit for hours working out how best to win a race under various conditions. As he rode in a race he always knew what all the other jockeys and horses were doing and what they were capable of doing. He seemed to inspire his horses with his own determination and will to win. He may be said to have forced the very maximum exertion out of every mount in his determination to win at all costs. He was somewhat ruthless with his brother jockeys who hindered him or got in his way during a race, as the following anecdote shows :

An owner was running a horse with an apprentice riding in a race in which Archer was also engaged. The owner knew that the lad had a stone in hand and gave him instructions that he could not help winning but that as he did not want the form exposed the lad was to win it by as narrow a margin as possible. To the owner's amazement and anger he saw his jockey make all the running and win by several lengths. "Well sir," explained the trembling lad, "I heard Mr. Harcher say to another jockey at the starting post, 'We'll soon have this young —— over the rails!' so I thought I'd better come away as fast as I could!" The lad was acquitted with honour.

Bend Or's Derby was probably as good a race as Archer ever rode.

A few weeks previously his arm had been badly damaged by a noted savage of a horse called Muley Edris, and the arm was supported by an iron and practically useless when he got up on Bend Or in the paddock at Epsom. Rossiter on Robert the Devil was so far in front coming into the straight that the bookmakers were taking 10–1 on him. Gradually Archer on Bend Or closed the gap but two lengths from the post Robert the Devil was still in front. Then Archer made one of his brilliantly timed last-minute efforts, with legs and arm he seemed to lift Bend Or past the post. Nobody knew until the numbers went up who had won, the ring laying five to one that Archer had not got up. When his number went up there was such a roar of cheering that had never been heard at Epsom to that day. Many people blamed Rossiter for not having won, and as the two returned through the crowd to the paddock Archer heard a bystander proclaim against Rossiter's riding of the race. Turning on him he said sharply, "Don't say that, it isn't true. The lad rode as well as any lad could, but met a better horse!"

Mr. Wyndham B. Portman, the then proprietor of *Horse and Hound*, writing under the nom de plume of "Audax," wrote in that paper on Saturday, 13th November, 1886:

The one absorbing topic of conversation in Turf circles this week has been the melancholy death of Fred Archer, and never have I noted more signs of genuine grief than when it transpired at Albert Gate on Monday afternoon that he had passed away by his own hand whilst under the influence of delirium. So much has been written on the subject that I will not fill our pages with a lengthened account of his career, but briefly express my own unfeigned sorrow for the death of the brightest ornament of his profession, and one who made many friends by his undeviating truthfulness, his modesty under adulation which might have turned weaker heads, and his gentlemanly bearing in every relation to life.

As a jockey I never saw his superior, and I have seen James Robinson, Sam Chifney, Frank Butler, Alfred Day, Custance, Tom French, Tom

Aldcroft, and the immortal George Fordham show their brilliant skill in the pigskin. Many others have shown as grand horsemanship in special instances, but as an all-round jockey Fred Archer had no equals in my opinion. One main secret of his success was his undeviating attention to business, always seeing that his weight was right, his horse properly saddled, and that he reached the post in good time.

The starters will miss him, as he set a bright example of submission to those in authority, never attempting to take advantage until the flag was dropped ; yet so skilful was he, so keenly did he watch the starter's movements, that he knew when to go, and won scores of races by his judgement at the starting post. In the actual race too, how different was his riding to that of the many headless horsemen that call themselves jockeys, and I pause to think how many races I have seen him snatch out of the fire, and drop a tear of unfeigned sorrow to think I shall never see his brilliant horsemanship again.

STEPHEN DONOGHUE

Was born at Warrington, Lancashire, in 1884.

Determined to become a great jockey he ran away from home and obtained a job as a stable lad with Dobson Peacock under a false name. Tod Sloan was the idol upon whom he modelled his riding. He rode his first winner in France in 1905, and from there to Ireland, where he was champion jockey, 1909, before returning to England to make his name, heading the list of winning jockeys from 1914–1922 inclusive, and sharing the honour in 1923 with E. C. Elliott. Donoghue rode in 14,008 races and won 1844, the Derby six times, including a hat-trick, and the Queen Alexandra Stakes at Ascot on old Brown Jack for six consecutive years. Rode the winner and a third out of his only two rides over hurdles. Died in 1945.—P. B.

MY HAT-TRICK DERBY WINNER :

Papyrus did not run between winning the Chester Vase and the Derby, but his final gallop gave me great confidence in him. On the morning of the Derby he reminded me of Humorist. I was, as usual, up with the sun and went down to Epsom to give him a little spin on the course. Just like Humorist on Derby day, he was full of spirits and he danced along in an exercise canter with his ears pricked, thoroughly in love with life. I had made my plan of campaign. I would move up to a good position, fifth or sixth, early in the race, and after that I would tackle Tattenham in my customary way and hope for the best on the home stretch. But no Derby day seems to go without some excitement where I am concerned. In the first race a stone or clod of hard earth was flung up by the horse in front of me and hit me in the left eye. It hurt like the very devil, and when, after the second race, I came back into the unsaddling enclosure my eye was completely closed and throbbing painfully. I was taken quickly to the ambulance room and the doctor examined it. "I'll have to lance this, Steve." "No, Doctor," I said. "Don't touch it until after I have won the Derby. You can do what you like with it after that." I would not have it touched, although it was my left eye, my rails eye, and I had to go round Tattenham Corner without the use of it ! I was drawn eighteen ! A very good draw. Eighteen was the outside all but one. I now trusted Papyrus to get me the position I wanted in the first four furlongs. In the paddock I saw Papyrus looking calm and collected and wonderfully fit. I was also impressed with the looks and fitness of Pharos. Papyrus went down to the post full of fire and spirit. I still felt very confident in his ability to make me the first jockey ever to win three Derbys in succession. I knew that Pharos was the horse I had to expect a challenge from. He belonged to my kind friend Lord Derby, whom many thought had his best chance of winning the race that bore his name and had evaded him for so long. The start was good except that Parth stuck his toes into the ground as the tapes went up and lost a few lengths. Knockando went away at a great bat, making the running, and I was pleased at the good pace which was being set. Knockando took the rails, but I tucked in behind him, handy, with Ellangowan on my right and Pharos just behind. There was a lot of mist about and they probably could not see us clearly from the grandstand. At the top of the hill I saw what I was waiting for. The pace had been too much for Knockando and his bolt was shot. I dashed across and took his place on the rails. My plan was working out like clockwork. Down the hill we dashed, and Papyrus acting on the sloping ground perfectly I took him round Tattenham Corner fast, and he was as balanced as though on the straight. Once past Tattenham Corner I sent my game little mount into the lead, and then came the challenge I had been expecting. Pharos, ridden by Gardner, was lying handy to me, and with his horse beautifully balanced he sent him up to me. Now was the moment to test that stamina, that gameness ; to trust that pluck which had caused me to let go my retainer and put my trust in this little brown horse. Pharos drew level with me. He was going splendidly. His jockey asked him for more and, gamely, he gave it. Neck and neck we raced until we were only two furlongs from home. Papyrus was doing all

I was asking of him. I could feel him going smoothly under me, and I felt a wonderful affection for him as he stayed on. Then Pharos crept ahead of me, half a length perhaps, but he headed me. Now was the moment which meant everything to me. I had to ask the courageous little animal for more, though the pace was gruelling. I asked him with my hands and my knees, and with glorious pluck, superb courage, the little fellow quickened his stride in an effort that made me love him. Knowing that everything depended on the next furlong, I called on him for more and more, helping him all I could with my hands. He gave all that I asked with incomparable courage. He drew up on Pharos and pegged him back. He went into the lead and there he stayed, galloping as straight and as true as a gun-barrel, until we swept past the post to win by a length from as game a horse as ever looked through a bridle. Brave, gallant little Papyrus ! I was tingling from head to foot with happiness. He had proved my faith in him as only a game horse will ; he had given me a record never held by a jockey before, and, if possible, he had made me love and admire a thoroughbred horse more than ever before. As I patted his sweating neck I glanced at Pharos while we rode back to the unsaddling enclosure. All honour to the grand fellow for his brilliant fight, and honouring him is honouring Papyrus. As I approached the enclosure, my one open eye wet with excitement, the first person to come up to me was Lord Derby. The sight of his kind, beaming smile, his ungrudging praise, made me almost sorry that I had beaten his splendid horse which had come so near to winning. But he laughed as he held out his hand to me and remarked : "Stephen, if they had kept you in the ambulance room another half an hour I should have won the Derby." What a sportsman and what a gentleman ! Win or lose he is never different. I unsaddled my hat-trick horse and weighed out. . . .

BROWN JACK :

I don't think I have ever spent such a strange weekend as that in which my old pal Brown Jack won the Alexandra Stakes for the sixth and last time. In some ways it was the happiest weekend of my life. I went down to the post on the old fellow full of confidence. because, although everyone, from Alfie, his stable lad, to Ivor Anthony, his trainer, was desperately nervous that the old horse might fail the last time, I knew him so well and was so fond of him that I felt certain he would finish again if necessary with one of his old-fashioned head victories. Also, though it may sound strange when it is remembered that the horse was then ten years old, he seemed to me to be going better than ever before in his long career. My son Pat was riding the faithful old Mail Fist from the same stable. I told him to make the pace a good gallop. If you are riding a horse with stamina like that of old Brown Jack, in a long-distance race like the Alexandra Stakes, it is essential to make the pace a good gallop, or some horse with less stamina and a good turn of speed will nurse himself throughout the race and then come up on you at the distance and, possibly, do you out of a race that should be yours. Well, I told Pat to make it a good gallop and to keep on the rails so that everyone would have to go round him to get in front. The gate went up and away went Mail Fist in his usual fly-away fashion right into the lead. Brown Jack got away beautifully and was soon going in his customary easy style. I just sat up there, keeping him balanced and handy, watching what the others were going to do in their efforts to defeat my old friend. Most of them seemed to think that Mail Fist might not really be making the pace fast enough, so one of them galloped up alongside him and even took the lead from him. I was just coming along nicely waiting for Pat to give me the signal that Mail Fist had finished making his helpful effort. We had done about a mile and a half when I saw that it was time for me to move up on the old champion. Pat was riding very close to the rails, so I came up smoothly on the off side and called to him that I was coming. I was nearly past him when I heard him shout " Daddy, Dad ! " Having been sent along, old Brown Jack was keen to carry on, and I was busy keeping him just as I wanted him, but when Pat shouted to me I looked over my shoulder, shouting, " What's the matter ? " Pat yelled back, " You're putting me over the rails," and sure enough Jack had cut it so fine that the poor lad was right up against the rails. I steadied Brown Jack and sent him on after the leaders. As we came into the straight he polished off one stubborn horse, and then went after Solatium in front. We battled along side by side for the best part of 100 yards. I know people on the stands must have been thinking that old Jack had at last met his match, but he had not. Solatium was dead game, but that 100 yards of Brown Jack at his best was too much for any horse, and slowly he fell back beaten. What happened after that only proves what a great old character Jack was. It had always been his custom to slow down after he had beaten all his opponents, knowing that they would not come again and once or twice I had had to work a bit to keep him going until the post was past. Here he was racing in the last race of his career. I had lost my whip some distance before the end of the race. Now no horse that was ever foaled was gamer than Brown Jack. He would not flinch from a gruelling finish, as threatened us in the last stages of that race ; in fact, he enjoyed that sort of finish. But as soon as I dropped my whip we had just got into the lead at the time—he seemed to know it and

The old boy had done it for the sixth year in succession.

immediately he began to show signs of shortening his stride. I talked to him very firmly. " Get on there, you old scamp," I said to him. " Get along there, you know damn well I have dropped my whip but I won't stand for any monkey tricks and you know it. Get along there." And as I spoke to him I kept touching his side with my hand. He knew me and he knew the occasion and he battled on splendidly but as sure as my name's what it is, I am certain that that old rogue was laughing at me for dropping my whip and I know that he enjoyed giving me that fright. Just as he had done every time before, he pricked his ears as he approached the post and did his comic little dance—he always did this when he won—as he passed it. Never will I forget the roar of that crowd as long as I live. Ascot or no Ascot they went mad. I have never seen so many hats flung in the air, and I have never heard such shrieks of joy in my life. All my six Derbys faded before the reception that was awaiting Jack and myself as we set out to return to weigh in. I don't think I was ever so happy in my life as I was at that moment. Then as we approached the crowd the noise became something terrific. The old boy had done it for the sixth time in succession, and had made a record that was never likely to be beaten, and here he was in the middle of an enormous crowd, walking through them, submitting to their slaps and pats and hair removals like some pet pony among children. What an old hero and what an old gentleman. It was all so different from what I had expected. I had started out in the race with two false beards in my pocket—one for Jack and one for myself. I had intended if we won to put one beard on him and the other on myself before I returned to the paddock. I knew the sight of we two old warriors returning after the race like two old bearded men about to retire would have made the crowd laugh. But when the time came to do it I just could not go through with it. Perhaps I felt the occasion to be too great. Anyway, we struggled through the crowd, and Jack had lost half his tail long before we reached the enclosure. Then suddenly I noticed that the old fellow was pulling away to the left instead of going straight on to the unsaddling enclosure. He should have known his way to that enclosure ! He had been in there for years in succession. But he seemed to want to go off to the left. Knowing the old man seldom did anything without a reason, I dropped the reins and watched to see which way he would go. He swerved to the left and made his way through the crush. Then I saw what he had in mind. Pat was leading in his old pal, Mail Fist, who had broken down during the race. Brown Jack walked over to him and sniffed him, and he seemed to be saying : " Sorry, old fellow, here am I covered in glory and you have broken down. Never mind." Then he turned away from his friend and walked straight to the enclosure. But as we got to the opening in the enclosure an old woman with white hair stretched up to pat his neck. Like the gentleman he was, Jack stopped and lowered his head for her to stroke him, but it was not entirely a gesture of good manners for while she was patting his neck he was eating a bunch of flowers in her button hole. When he had finished he went on into the enclosure and I saw his trainer Ivor Anthony for the first time since the race had started. He had not seen it. He could not stand the suspense. He had sat behind the stands until the roars of the crowd told him that we had passed the winning post in the right order. A few minutes later the public part of the happiest day in my life was over. Brown Jack went back to his training quarters in a van on which someone had chalked the words " Brown Jack," and Alfie told me afterwards that they made the journey half an hour quicker than ever before, and were cheered in every traffic block in which they stopped. . . .

STEVE DONOGHUE'S TRIBUTE TO FRED REES :

But there have been great jumping jockeys who were not at a disadvantage with a flat-race jockey in a finish. The greatest jockey on the flat, over hurdles, or the stiffest steeplechase course during my time was Fred Rees. I remember at the very beginning of his career his riding in a flat race at Brighton. I had something to do with his riding there. The race resolved itself into a match between himself and Carslake. Carslake came to me before the race and asked me who Rees was. " Oh ! Just a ' flapper,' " I told him. A " flapper " is our name for an amateur.

It was one of the finest races I have ever seen. In the last furlong Carslake and Fred were riding neck and neck. There is no jockey riding who can give an ounce to Carslake in a finish ; he is a tremendous finisher. But Fred Rees beat him a head, though he was then at the beginning of his career.

" Nice sort of ' flapper ' you gave me, Steve," Carslake said afterwards, laughingly. But Carslake had nothing to be ashamed of, as Rees went on to prove himself the most brilliant all-round horseman of his time. I have never heard anyone dispute that opinion.

STEVE DONOGHUE : *Donoghue Up !*

FAMOUS RIDES IN FACT AND FICTION

To witch the world with noble horsemanship.
SHAKESPEARE.

DICK TURPIN

I have no wish to join in the perennial controversy on Dick Turpin and his supposed ride to York beyond mentioning the ride of another man on that road which seems to bear too close a resemblance to Ainsworth's romantic tale to be purely coincidence. While there appears every reason to believe that an unprincipled rascal named Turpin did exist, and exist on the spoil of highway robberies, it seems improbable that he was the hero of any ride to York. Another highwayman, one named Nicks,* is said to have achieved something akin to, though less colourful and improbable than, the Turpin legend.

Nicks, it is related, having committed a highway robbery in the neighbourhood of Chatham, at four o'clock in the morning, set spurs to the mare he was riding and galloped off to Gravesend ; here, after some little delay, which he occupied in baiting the mare, he obtained a boat in which man and horse crossed to the Essex shore, and proceeded to Chelmsford, where the mare was baited again. Thence keeping as far as possible to side roads and the open country they travelled to Cambridge ; from here more by-roads brought them to Huntingdon, where an hour's rest was taken. Then, following the main road and maintaining a gallop most of the time, they managed to make York before the evening was far advanced. Nicks wasted no time but changed his clothes and went straight to the town bowling green, where among those present, he recognised none other than the Lord Mayor, whom he immediately accosted asking what time it was ; he received the reply that it was a quarter past eight, and thereon hung his alibi. When later he was tried for the robbery he was acquitted on the Lord Mayor's evidence of his having been in York at the time mentioned, as it was considered impossible for him to have been so far away as the scene of the theft in the time, although the man he had robbed swore Nicks was the culprit.

HUGH MCCAUSLAND : *The Horse*, Vol. XII

Nicks then established himself as a horse dealer, in the neighbourhood of York and all went well until he was involved in a shady deal and the customer had him up for sharp practice. He was convicted and gaoled. It was then that the truth of his previous Chatham robbery and his amazing ride came to light.—P. B.

* Nevison is said to have been his correct name, it was as Nicks that he was best known—possibly the original " nickname " !

A Post-boy, Jack Story, of the Crown at Penrith, once rode 108 miles—twice to Carlisle and back and once to Keswick—in a day, when he was past seventy. Such a ride made no difference to him and he ultimately died at the age of eighty-five.

THE DRUID : *Post and Paddock*, 1856.

TSCHIFFELY'S RIDE

I rode some 10,000 miles in two and a half years. From Argentina I came North, over cold, barren 16,000-foot ranges ; then down into steamy jungles, across the Isthmus of Panama, up through Central America and Mexico, and so to the United States. I reached Washington with the same two horses with which I started—ponies that were fifteen and sixteen years old when my ride began. Remote from cities and seaports—far from white men's haunts—ran much of my lonely trail. One night camp might be pitched far from any human habitation ; again, I ate and slept with ancient Indian tribes in stone villages older than the Incas. Of high adventures, hair-breadth escapes, and deeds of daring, there were few ; yet in all the annals of exploration I doubt if any traveller, not excepting Marco Polo himself, had more leisure than I to see and understand the people, the animals and plant life of the countries traversed. . . .

What is particularly gratifying to me is the knowledge that I have been able to prove that the Argentine Criollo (Creole) horse is worthy of the reputation he has always held among the few that really know him, namely, that of being second to none for continuous hard work under any conditions. My two pals, " Mancha " and " Gato," have shown powers of resistance to heat, cold, hunger, and every hardship imaginable that have surprised even the most sanguine admirers of the breed, and Dr. Emilio Solanet, who presented them to me, must indeed feel proud of them.

THE ROLLING PAMPAS :

At another estancia I had the opportunity of witnessing a " domada " or horse-breaking. The " domador " (breaker) was occupied in taming a troop of " potros " (broncos), from 3 to 4 years old, some of them as wild as cats ; he was a tall, slim young fellow, about 24 years of age, dark and handsome, and concerned himself solely with the riding. The catching and saddling were in the hands of two assistants. These entered the corral, lasso in hand, and with shouts and waving of the rope caused the horses to gallop wildly round and round until the object of their search was clear of the others, when the rope was dropped on his neck with unerring aim. It was almost uncanny the way in which the horse that was wanted divined their intentions. He would twist and turn about, always keeping two or three other horses between himself and the men, while the rest appeared to be helping him deliberately. However, in the long run he was caught and the lasso immediately whipped about a "palenque" (post) in the middle of the corral. As he kicked and struggled his legs were roped and he came to earth with a crash. While he was down the "bocado" was slipped into his mouth. This is used instead of a bit and is simply a strip of raw-hide tied firmly round his lower jaw and to which the reins are attached. He was then allowed to rise, but his hind legs were roped together, one foreleg slung up and his head tied close to the palenque. Then one of the assistants saddled him while the other looked after the ropes. The cinches were tightened until the animal looked like an early Victorian belle, and when all was ready he was dragged out cautiously on three legs, the foreleg still slung up, into the open field. Even with only three legs to walk on he could spare one to kick with, and the men were extremely careful. Once in the potrero the domador mounted, the ropes were cast off and then the band began to play. Plunging, kicking, bucking, the maddened potro strove to rid himself of his rider, but each buck only resulted in a vicious whack from the broad raw-hide lash of the "rebenque" (whip). Changing his tactics he tore at full speed, and now found another horse on each side of him, whose riders frustrated any attempts he made to get to the fence where he might brush this burden from his back. Round and round the field they galloped, the domador occasionally forcing him to slow down by hauling with all his strength on the reins, at other times encouraging him to dash along with shouts and lashes. Finally, he was brought to a standstill; the first lesson was over. The rider dismounted and calmly lit a cigarette without—as far as I could see—the slightest sign of a tremor in his hand, and waited for the next animal to be saddled.

IN THE HISTORICAL TOWN OF QUERETARO MEXICO:

Among other things a "jaripeo" (rodeo) was given in the local bull-ring where I again witnessed some daring and skill. The most remarkable feat performed was when a charro tied his rope, ending in a running noose, around his neck, and, when thus tied, roped and threw a wild horse. The slightest mistake in judgement would probably have been fatal, but even after having done the trick once, he twice successfully repeated it. To make things more difficult, he did all manner of fancy twirling and skipping through the rope before lassoing the animal, which he did without stopping to take aim, bringing the horse down in a flash.

IN THE IMPORTANT TOWN OF SAN LUIS POTOSI, MEXICO :

The local charros gave a splendid exhibition of their skill in the bull-ring and one of them performed a trick that I had never before seen or heard of. Riding his horse this charro chased a wild mare and, when he had the chance, he jumped on to her back. When she had unsuccessfully tried every vicious trick in her repertoire to shake him off, the charro spurred her into a gallop, and then called his tame and splendidly trained saddle-horse, which immediately came alongside the racing mare, whereupon the man jumped gracefully back into the saddle. This trick is named "Paso de la muerte" (death pass), and is one of the finest pieces of horsemanship I have ever seen performed, for not only does it require a great rider, but a perfect training of the saddle-horse, a thing about which the average cowboy, charro, or gaucho horse-breaker knows very little. It is one thing to be a "bronco-buster" and another a horseman, and the mixture of the two is rare to find.

LANDSLIDES, A DETOUR AND A MOUNTAIN STORM :

We had crossed some giddy and wobbly hanging bridges before, but here we came to the worst I had ever seen or ever wish to see again. Even without horses the crossing of such bridges is apt to make anybody feel cold ripples down the back, and, in fact, many people have to be blindfolded and strapped on stretchers to be carried across. Spanning a wild river the bridge looked like a long, thin hammock swung high up from one rock to another. Bits of rope, wire and fibre held the rickety structure together, and the floor was made of sticks laid crosswise and covered with some coarse fibre matting to give a foothold, and to prevent slipping that would inevitably prove fatal. The width of this extraordinary piece of engineering was no more than four feet, and its length must have been roughly one hundred and fifty yards. In the middle the thing sagged down like a slack rope.

I went to examine it closely, and the very sight of it made me feel giddy, and the thought of what might easily happen produced a feeling in my stomach as if I had swallowed a block of ice. For a while I hesitated, and then

I decided to chance it, for there was no other alternative but to return to Ayacucho and there wait for the dry season. I unsaddled the horses, and giving the Indian the lead line I made signs to him to go ahead with Mancha first. Knowing the horse well, I caught him by the tail and walked behind talking to him to keep him quiet. When we stepped on the bridge he hesitated for a moment, then he sniffed the matting with suspicion, and after examining the strange surroundings he listened to me and cautiously advanced. As we approached the deep sag in the middle, the bridge began to sway horribly, and for a moment I was afraid the horse would try to turn back, which would have been the end of him ; but no, he had merely stopped to wait until the swinging motion was less, and then he moved on again. I was nearly choking with excitement, but kept on talking to him and patting his haunches, an

It is one thing to be a "bronco-buster."

attention of which he was very fond. Once we started upwards after having crossed the middle, even the horse seemed to realise that we had passed the worst part, for now he began to hurry towards safety. His weight shook the bridge so much that I had to catch hold of the wires on the sides to keep my balance. Gato, when his turn came, seeing his companion on the other side, gave less trouble and crossed over as steadily as if he were walking along a trail. Once the horses were safely on the other side we carried over the packs and saddles.

A. F. Tschiffely: *Tschiffely's Ride.*

GATO AND MANCHA

Ridden by A. F. Tschiffely from Buenos Aires to Washington.

Who that has loved good horses
  But is thrilled by the thought of these
Who have striven with Nature's forces
  And mastered her armouries?
Come, drink to each game Criollo
  Who carried saddle and pack
On the road no horse will follow
  Till the gods have levelled the track!

Will. H. Ogilvie: *Saddles Again.*

MAZEPPA

A trampling troop; I see them come!
In one vast squadron they advance!
I strove to cry—my lips were dumb.
The steeds rush on in plunging pride;
But where are they the reins to guide?
A thousand horse—and none to ride!
With flowing tail, and flying mane,
Wide nostrils—never stretch'd by pain,
Mouths bloodless to the bit or rein,
And feet that iron never shod,
And flanks unscarr'd by spur or rod,
A thousand horse, the wild, the free,
Like waves that follow o'er the sea,
Came thickly thundering on,
As if our faint approach to meet;
The sight re-nerved my courser's feet,
A moment staggering, feebly fleet,
A moment, with a faint low neigh,
He answer'd, and then fell;
With gasps and glazing eyes he lay,
And reeking limbs immoveable,
His first and last career is done!
On came the troop—they saw him stoop,
They saw me strangely bound along
His back with many a bloody thong:
They stop—they start—they snuff the air,
Gallop a moment here and there,
Approach, retire, wheel round and round,
Then plunging back with sudden bound,
Headed by one black mighty steed,
Who seem'd the patriarch of his breed,
Without a single speck or hair
Of white upon his shaggy hide;
They snort—they foam—neigh—swerve aside,
And backward to the forest fly,
By instinct, from a human eye.—
They left me there to my despair,
Link'd to the dead and stiffening wretch,
Whose lifeless limbs beneath me stretch . . .

BYRON

Mazeppa was born in Kiev in 1644 and became page to John Casimir, King of Poland. A nobleman of the King's court discovering his wife's intrigue with Mazeppa caused the latter to be bound naked to a wild horse and left to his fate. Byron tells us in his lively and spirited poem, of Mazeppa's adventures and feelings on his involuntary ride, chased by a pack of wolves, and meeting the herd of wild horses. History relates that Mazeppa was rescued by a Cossack family and became secretary to the Cossack Hetman Samoilowitch whom he succeeded in 1687. He assisted Peter the Great against Turkey, and was made by him Prince of the Ukraine. Later he plotted against Peter with Charles XII but they were defeated at Poltava. Mazeppa fled to Bender, where he died in 1709.—P. B.

THE CHARGE OF THE LIGHT BRIGADE BALACLAVA, 25TH OCTOBER 1854

"Forward, the Light Brigade!"
Was there a man dismay'd?
Not tho' the soldier knew
  Some one had blunder'd:
Their's not to make reply,
Their's not to reason why,
Their's but to do and die:
Into the valley of Death
  Rode the six hundred.

TENNYSON

The circumstances leading up to this famous charge have been somewhat obscured by the passage of time, but that it was the result of a wrongly interpreted command is established as a certainty.

The popularly accepted facts are as follows; Lord Raglan, the Allied Commander-in-Chief observed from his Headquarters situated in a position overlooking the scene of operations, that the Russians were preparing to remove some British guns they had recently captured from the Turks on Causeway Heights, a position to the South of where the Light Brigade had been drawn up for a considerable time restlessly awaiting the order to be brought into action. An order was immediately dispatched to Lord Lucan the Commander of the Cavalry Division comprising the Light and Heavy

Brigades (the latter having already distinguished themselves on this memorable day). This order was carried by an aide, Captain Nolan, and read as follows, " Lord Raglan wishes the Cavalry to advance rapidly to the front and try to prevent the enemy carrying away the guns—Immediate." To this order Lucan who was not in the commanding position enjoyed by the C.-in-C., and was therefore uncertain as to its exact meaning, raised a bewildered protest, whereupon Nolan, fretting at the prolonged inactivity of the Brigade and apparent stupidity of its Commander, replied, " Lord Raglan's orders are that the Cavalry shall attack immediately." (Nolan's excitability, and impetuosity, may have been the cause of his substituting the word " attack " in place of the order " advance "). To this, Lucan burst out, " Attack, Sir ! attack what ? what guns, Sir ? " Nolan now pointed vaguely down the valley at the foot of which were the massed Russian batteries of 30 guns, and replied, " There my Lord is your enemy, there are your guns." Lord Lucan rode over to the Commander of the Light Brigade, Lord Cardigan, and reluctantly gave the order that was to start the historical and glorious charge.

At 11.10 the 678 officers and O.R.s of the Light Brigade moved off behind Lord Cardigan in three lines, the 17th Lancers commanded by Captain Morris, distinguished by the forage cap he was wearing, and the 13th Light Dragoons, forming the first line, the 11th Hussars the second line, and the third line under Lord George Paget who was smoking a large cigar, the 4th Light Dragoons, and the 8th Hussars commanded by Colonel Shewall.

A colourful personality in the shape of Private Veigh, Butcher of the 17th Lancers, was among the 139 men in the ranks of that famous Regiment. Veigh was engaged in his daily task when news of the coming charge reached him. He immediately buckled over his bloodstained smock the accoutrements of a dead dragoon lying nearby, and grabbing a stray horse rode up in time to fall in in the ranks of his Regiment carrying his meat axe in lieu of a lance.

After a short distance had been covered, Captain Nolan, who was riding with the 17th Lancers, alongside his friend, Captain Morris, is believed to have realised his fatal error in direction, as spurring his horse into a gallop he broke from the leading ranks and dashed madly across the front of Lord Cardigan shouting, gesticulating and waving his sword in the direction of Causeway Heights. Before he had gone far and before his shouts were understood the first shell from the Russian batteries burst overhead and a fragment laid bare his heart. Nolan remained in the saddle, but his sword arm dropped and his horse swung round and galloped down the interval between the regiments, where uttering his last agonising cry he dropped lifeless to the ground, first casualty of the bloody debacle.

To quote C. E. Vulliamy from his book *Crimea* :

Those on the high bluff with Raglan at the head of the valley saw the Light Brigade, in rapidly receding lines, riding to annihilation. Surely Cardigan would presently wheel to his right, ascending the Causeway. He was clearly discernible, on a chestnut horse with two white legs and red " overalls," but he went on, leading his brigade towards a battery in line, between the flanking fire of the hills. General Bosquet turned in dismay to Layard. " *C'est magnifique*," he cried, " *mais ce n'est pas la guerre—c'est de la folie !* " Folly it was indeed ; heroic folly ; superb discipline under the orders of incurable stupidity ; a sight moving men to tears, laughter, rage and admiration. It was now too late for Lucan to stop or divert the charge : he began to move the heavies forward in support. At the same time Canrobert ordered the 4th Chasseurs d'Afrique, commanded by d'Allonville to attack the Russian batteries on the Fedukhine heights—that is, on the left or northern side of the valley. Parallel to the front of Cardigan's charging brigade was a line of twelve brass cannon. With an echoing roar these guns fired simultaneously at the advancing horsemen, and a dense white layer of smoke began to spread over the field. Infantry and artillery on the hills, at a range of rather less than a quarter of a mile, were pouring out their deadly converging streams of shot or grape, rifle-balls or canister. The clatter of musketry was audible, like an irregular tapping of great drumsticks, above the pealing crash of the batteries. Horsemen and horses fell, some dead, some miserably wounded, lying still or painfully dragging themselves on the grass. But the narrowing ranks drew together, always in line—so perfect was their discipline, even in this roaring hell. And even as the charge became faster Cardigan remembered his drill-book. He stretched out his level sword across the bosom of Captain White of the Lancers, who was advancing too quickly.

In the last line, under Paget, the riderless horses, coming back from the leading squadrons, were the cause of unavoidable disorder. The officers were busily keeping their troopers, as well as they could, in their proper formation. Paget still kept his cigar between his teeth. " Close in to the centre . . . back a little, Trooper Brown . . . keep up, the right flank . . . steady ! " More and more the riderless horses were pressing in upon them, " in every state of mutilation." " They made dashes at me," Paget records in his journal, " some advancing with me a considerable distance, at one time as many as five on my right and two on my left, cringing in on me and positively squeezing me . . . my overalls being a mass of blood from their gory flanks (they nearly upset me several times, and I had . . . to use my sword to . . .

He stretched out his level sword across the bosom of Captain White of the Lancers.

rid myself of them)." The first line, or what remained of it, was now galloping down upon the battery. In rear of the guns a mass of cavalry and infantry was drawn up across the narrow end of the valley and under the hills. Cardigan's incredible men, already a mere handful were charging an army in position. At a range of about 80 yards a few hastily reloaded guns in the battery fired a salvo. The front of the Light Brigade now consisted only of some fifty to sixty riders. Cheering impetuously these men disappeared in the smoke of the final volley. Cardigan himself gave a meticulous professional estimate of his exact speed as he rode into the battery ; it was, he declared, about seventeen miles an hour. His troopers came in behind him. They could see dimly the gleam of brass guns in the whirl of smoke, and a shaken mass of artillery-men or cavalry. Without any endeavour to rally or command his brigade, the leader rode on into the tumult.

C. E. VULLIAMY : *Crimea.*

At this point the gallant Captain Morris found that in the smoke and confusion he had ridden round the left flank of the Russian battery, and was faced by a horde of Cossack cavalry. A few survivors of his regiment being with him, he led them straight into the enemy. After receiving two sabre cuts and a lance wound he was forced to surrender, but later escaped, wounded and exhausted he staggered back to fall near the dead body of his friend Nolan. Another officer of this regiment, Sir William Gordon, received no less than five sabre wounds in the head, and rode back with his head along his horse's neck, vainly attempting to keep the blood from his eyes. The extraction and withdrawal of the remnants of the Brigade added to the general confusion, and a charge was made on their flank by the Russian cavalry. This was seen by Colonel Shewall commanding the 8th Hussars. Wheeling the remnants of his Regiment round he dispersed the enemy attack, but not without sustaining further heavy losses.

By 11.35 the Light Brigade was no longer in existence. Only 195 men had managed to cover the 1½ miles back up that ghastly valley to answer the roll call. One hundred and thirteen men had been killed and 134 wounded, while 475 horses had been either killed in the battle or had to be shot immediately afterwards.—P. B.

The noblest blood of England
Around those guns had flowed
Ere, dealing death like victors round,
The remnant backwards rode.

HELEN MACGREGOR.

THE CHARGE OF THE HEAVY BRIGADE

The glorious failure of the Charge of the Light Brigade seems to have overshadowed the feat of the Heavy Brigade who earlier in the same day had been successful in one of the greatest cavalry charges in English history. The charge of the Heavy Brigade against a Russian cavalry corps three times its strength was as well ordered and successful as the later charge by the Light Brigade was ill-advised and disastrous.

The three regiments making up the Heavy Brigade were the Royals (English), Scots Greys (Scottish), and The Inniskilling Dragoons (Irish), whilst the 4th and 5th Dragoon Guards were added and subsequently dashed up in support.—P. B.

O mad for the charge and the battle were we,
When our own good redcoats sank from sight,
Like drops of blood in a dark-gray sea,
And we turn'd to each other, whispering, all dismay'd,

. . . . . .

Glory to each and to all, and the charge that they made!
Glory to all the three hundred, and all the Brigade!

TENNYSON.

THE LANDLORD'S TALE

PAUL REVERE'S RIDE

Listen, my children, and you shall hear
Of the midnight ride of Paul Revere,
On the eighteenth of April, in Seventy-five;
Hardly a man is now alive
Who remembers that famous day and year.

He said to his friend, "If the British march
By land or sea from the town to-night,
Hang a lantern aloft in the belfry arch
Of the North Church tower as a signal light,—
One, if by land, and two, if by sea;
And I on the opposite shore will be,
Ready to ride and spread the alarm
Through every Middlesex village and farm,
For the country folk to be up and to arm."

. . . .

So through the night rode Paul Revere;
And so through the night went his cry of alarm
To every Middlesex village and farm,—
A cry of defiance and not of fear,
A voice in the darkness, a knock at the door,
And a word that shall echo for evermore!
For, borne on a night-wind of the Past.
Through all our history, to the last,
In the hour of darkness and peril and need,
The people will waken and listen to hear
The hurrying hoof-beats of that steed,
And the midnight message of Paul Revere.

LONGFELLOW.

1775. The war in which the North American colonies rebelled against British domination. The British man-of-war *Somerset* was anchored in a bay off the province of Middlesex. Paul Revere was on the far side of the bay at Charlestown and arranged with a friend to signal to him the British movements, so that the American colonists might be warned in time to prepare for action. It was this timely warning that enabled the American colonists to win.—P. B.

EXTRAORDINARY MATCH BY GEO. OSBALDESTON, ESQUIRE.

This match was performed on Saturday, 5th Nov. 1831, on the Newmarket round course for a bet of a Thousand Guineas, Col. Charritie betting Mr. Osbaldeston that he did not perform the distance on horseback of 200 miles in 10 hours, the number of horses being unlimited. Various bye bets to a great amount were also made, one party betting ten hundred to one that Mr. Osbaldeston did not accomplish the task in 9 hours. The distance was performed in gallant style in 8 hours and 42 mins. including the time for mounting, dismounting and refreshments. The greater part of the day was very unfavourable, being very stormy and attended with heavy showers.

So much was written at the time about my ride at Newmarket when I did 200 miles in 8 hrs and 42 min. there is not much left to be said on the subject ; but a description of some of the horses and the circumstances connected with the match may not be uninteresting. . . . The match came off on the Saturday in the Houghton Meeting. Of course I was at Newmarket at the commencement of the meeting and had finished my training there . . . the match came off on the Round Course ; but in order to make it the 4 miles, which had been measured, I had to ride close to the ditch to the stand, instead of keeping the racecourse. I changed horses every 4 miles, finishing at the stand. I only rode the hunters or hacks once, but I rode the inferior racehorses twice and the superior ones three and some of them four times. Tranby, the property of Mr. Gully, carried me 16 miles in thirty-two and a half minutes, an extraordinary performance considering the weight which as I have said was 11 st. A black horse belonging to Mr. Sowerby always threw his jockey off at the end of the race, unless someone caught hold of his head, the instant he pulled up—he was very near serving me the same trick. Another horse called Ikey Solomon belonging to Mr. Nash, of balloon notoriety, was a vicious brute. There is a plantation along the left-hand side of the Round Course going out, and a rather hollow, firm track, close to it, which Buckle, the celebrated jockey, advised me to keep to, and I did. Without the least notice Ikey put his head down, and in a moment was bolting into the plantation where I must have been knocked off; but at that instant I tumbled off without hurting myself. I had placed 2 men on horseback at different points in case any of the horses tired or any accident occurred; it so happened that one of them was not 20 yards from me when I fell, and he came up in time to catch my friend Ikey, and I remounted and rode him the rest of the distance.

After riding 120 miles I stopped for eight minutes, during which time I ate and drank as much as I could; I was galloping one side of the ditch and the legitimate racing was going on on the other side, and many got on top of it, which enabled them to see both performances at the same time. A great many witnessed the match notwithstanding the races.

The two Chifneys, Sam and William, trainer and jockey, and some others galloped into the town with me down the street to the Rutland Arms Inn. I had just an hour and a half to spare before dinner, and went into a warm bath; after which Harry England, a good friend of mine, rubbed me all over with oils, and I got between the blankets, but did not sleep. I got up, dressed and joined my friends at dinner—we kept it up till two o'clock next morning.

I believe I could have ridden 300 miles in the same proportionate time, as I was not the least fatigued at the end of the match; but perhaps few will be able to believe this assertion. The soles of my feet were very sore next day, also my knees.

Squire Osbaldeston, His Autobiography: Edited by E. J. CUMMING.

Sir Tatton Sykes and the great jockey Frank Buckle (won 5 Derbys, 2 St. Legers and 9 Oaks) were the Squire's only rivals in horseback endurance. The latter rode his last race on one side of the ditch while the Squire was completing his great match on the other and was there to cheer him as he finished on Tranby, and making some remark to the effect that though he was fifteen years older he could ride farther and longer, was very nearly challenged to the proof. "To ride for twenty-five days, or till either of them dropped," were the terms which the public proposed for the match. As a feat of human endurance the one most nearly approaching the Squire's was that performed on 29th April 1745, thus described in the *Gentleman's Magazine*:

"Mr. Cooper Thornhill, innkeeper at Stilton, set out from thence at 4 o'clock this morning to ride to London, and came to the King's Arms over against Shoreditch Church ten minutes before eight. He turned back immediately for Stilton and from thence came again in good spirit to Shoreditch, the whole being 213 miles, which he was to perform with several horses in 15 hours for a considerable bett of his own money and large sums laid by Gentlemen."

"Naked she went, to clothe the naked."

LEIGH HUNT.

Lady Godiva, the subject of a legend, first mentioned in the writings of Roger of Wendover, was the wife of Leofric, Earl of Mercia. About 1040 in order to save Coventry from the exactions of her husband, she agreed to his harsh terms that she ride naked through the town in the light of midday. When this became known the people, out of the love they had for her, agreed to remain indoors behind drawn blinds so that her naked beauty went by unseen, except for the legendary "Peeping Tom," who spying through a small chink, was struck blind as he looked.—P. B.

HOW THEY BROUGHT THE GOOD NEWS FROM GHENT TO AIX

I sprang to the stirrup, and Joris, and he;
I galloped, Dirck galloped, we galloped all three;
"Good Speed!" cried the Watch, as the gate-bolts undrew;
"Speed!" echoed the wall to us galloping through;
Behind, shut the postern, the lights sank to rest,
And into the midnight we galloped abreast.

. . . . . .

And all I remember is, friends flocking round
As I sat with his head 'twixt my knees on the ground,
And no voice but was praising this Roland of mine,
As I poured down his throat our last measure of wine,
Which (the burgesses voted by common consent)
Was no more than his due who brought good news from Ghent.

ROBERT BROWNING.

Probably the news of the pacification of Ghent in 1578 when the Low Countries were at war with Spain. Aix is Aix-la-Chapelle. By this the citizens gained momentary advantage over the Spanish garrison. There is no historical record of the news being brought on horseback, only the imagination of Browning who drew upon his earlier experiences, passing through the Low Countries on his way to Russia in 1834, which had made him familiar with the route and the cities on the way.—P. B.

The race for the Grand National of 1921 was memorable for the amount of grief occasioned. Every single horse except the winner, Shaun Spadah, coming down. Turkey Buzzard, the top weight, fell at Becher's the second time round, and again at the next two fences, his plucky rider, Captain Bennett, managed to get back into the saddle each time, although he said after the race that he only remembered having had one fall! Gallant as was Captain Bennett's achievement, possibly the most courageous and determined action ever seen at Aintree was that of Mr. Harry Brown in the same race: riding his own horse, The Bore, he came into the last fence but one, behind the winner Shaun Spadah. The Bore fell heavily. Mr. Brown dragged the bridle off as he fell, and broke his collar bone. Exhausted as he was, dizzy with the pain, plastered with mud, and unable to raise his arm, his horse beaten and without a bridle, somehow he managed to get back into the saddle and set the old horse going again into a canter, and so over the last fence somehow, and past the winning post to take second place, though only just in front of All White who had fallen out in the country and been remounted. The cheering that greeted the gallant old horse and its plucky and great-hearted rider was just as loud and as long as had been accorded the winner.—P. B.

THE MIDNIGHT STEEPLECHASE

The steam of their steeds,
Like a mist of the meads,
Veiled the moon in a curtain of cloud.
And the stars so bright
Shuddered in light
As the unhallowed troop in their shadowy shroud,
Galloping, whooping, and yelling aloud,
Fast and unfailing, and furious in flight,
Rattled on like a hailstorm, and vanished in night.

ANON.

There are many versions as to the authenticity and the facts of the midnight steeplechase, it being generally supposed to have taken place near Ipswich on a certain night in December 1803, being the outcome of a cavalry subaltern's challenge after dinner in the mess at Ipswich where he was stationed—no regiment officially claims being the one concerned. Another version is that the race originated somewhere on the Thames near Maidenhead, being organised at short notice by the Hell Fire Club.—P. B.

RIDING TO HOUNDS

No colour like red.
 No sport like fox-hunting.
 R. S. SURTEES.

The soul of a horseman sings for joy of a hunting morn.

WILL. H. OGILVIE.

THE FOXHOUND

. . . Next to a Greek statue, I say, I know few such combinations of grace and strength as in a fine foxhound. It is the beauty of Theseus—light yet massive; and light not in spite of its masses, but on account of the perfect disposition of them. I do not care for grace in man, woman, or animal, which is obtained (as in the old German painters) at the expense of honest flesh and blood. It may be all very pure, and unearthly, and saintly, and what not; but it is not healthy; and therefore, it is not really High Art, let it call itself such as much as it likes. . . .

And all this has grown out of those foxhounds. Why not? Theirs is the sort of form which expresses to me what I want art to express—Nature not limited, but developed by high civilisation. The old savage idea of beauty was the lion, type of mere massive force. That was succeeded by an over-civilised ideal, say the fawn, type of delicate grace. By cunning breeding and choosing, through long centuries, man has combined both, and has created the foxhound, lion and fawn in one; just as he might create noble human beings; did he take half as much trouble about politics (in the true old sense of the word) as he does about fowls. Look at the old hound, who stands doubtful, looking up at his master for advice. Look at the severity, delicacy, lightness of every curve. His head is finer than a deer's; his hind legs tense as steel springs; his forelegs straight as arrows; and you see the depth of chest, the sweep of the loin, the breadth of paw, the mass of arm and thigh; and if you have an eye for form, look at the absolute majesty of attitude at this moment. Majesty is the only word for it. If he were six feet high, instead of twenty-three inches, with what animal on earth could you compare him?

Is it not a joy to see such a thing alive? It is to me at least. I should like to have one in my study all day long, as I would have a statue or a picture; and when Mr. Morrell gave (as they say) two hundred guineas for Hercules alone, I believe the dog was well worth the money, only to look at.

CHARLES KINGSLEY: *My Winter Garden*, 1858.

A HUNTSMAN'S PRAYER

An easterly wind and a lowering sky,
A straight-necked fox, with a scent breast high,
I pray for no more, unless a good start
At the tail of my hounds on the horse of my heart.

T. SCOTT ANDERSON: *Holloas from the Hills.*

"There, gentlemen," said the Squire to the assembled field at Kirby Gate, pointing to his famous bitch pack, nearly all by the renowned Furrier, "There they are, I have bred these beauties to please you. Ride over them if you can!"

SQUIRE OSBALDESTON: *The Quorn*, 1826.

Hark! The brave North-easter!
  Breast-high lies the scent,
On by holt and headland,
  Over heath and bent.
Chime, ye dappled darlings,
  Through the sleet and snow,
Who can over-ride you?
  Let the horses go!
Chime, ye dappled darlings,
  Down the roaring blast;
You shall see a fox die
  Ere an hour be past.

CHARLES KINGSLEY: *Ode to the North-East Wind.*

Yon sound's neither sheep-bell nor bark,
They're running—they're running, Go hark!

CHARLES KINGSLEY: *The Find*, 1856.

Lord Egremont's huntsman about 1773, on being asked the secret of breeding good foxhounds replied: "Stoody, stoody, stoody, be always stoodyin'. Ah say, be always stoodyin', stoody foxhuntin', stoody the pedigrees."

All nature looks balmy and gay ;
Let us join the glad throng that goes laughing along,
For we'll all go out hunting to-day.

FROM AN OLD SONG.

THE FIELD

And now appear, dim at first and distant, but brightening and nearing fast, many a right good fellow and many a right good horse. I know three or four of them, their private histories, the private histories of their horses : and could tell you many a good story of them : but shall not, being an English gentleman, and not an American Littérateur. They may not all be very clever, or very learned, or very anything except gallant men ; but they are all good enough company for me, or any one ; and each has his specialité for which I like him. That huntsman I have known for fifteen years, and sat many an hour beside his father's death-bed. I am godfather to that whip's child. I have seen the servants of the hunt, as I have seen the hounds, grow up round me for two generations, and I feel for them as old friends ; and like to look into their brave, honest, weather-beaten faces. That red coat there, I knew him when he was a schoolboy ; and now he is captain in the Guards, and won his Victoria Cross at Inkermann ; the bright green coat is the best farmer, as well as the hardest rider, for many a mile round ; one who plays, as he works, with all his might, and might have been a beau sabreur and colonel of Dragoons. So might that black coat, who now brews good beer, and stands up for the poor at the Board of Guardians, and rides like the green coat, as well as he works. That one, as clever and good as he is brave and simple, has stood by Napier's side in many an Indian fight ; that one won his Victoria at Delhi, and was cut up at Lucknow, with more than twenty wounds ; that one has—but what matter to you what each man is? Enough that each one can tell a good story, welcome one cheerfully, and give one out here, in the wild forest, the wholesome feeling of being at home among friends.

CHARLES KINGSLEY : *My Winter Garden.*

Better to hunt in fields for health unbought,
Than fee the doctor for a nauseous draught.

DRYDEN.

Dick Christian in his " Sporting Lectures " as narrated by " The Druid " in *Silk and Scarlet* referring to Thomas Assheton Smith says :

No man that ever came out of Leicestershire could beat Mr. Smith. . . .

It was a great speech of his, if ever he saw a horse refuse with his whips—*throw your heart over, and your horse will follow !*

He never rode fast at his fences. I've heard him say scores of times : " *When a man rides at fences a hundred miles an hour, depend on it, he funks.*"

He never made nothing of his leaps ; he'd turn round in his saddle over the biggest, when he was in the air, to look for his hounds. He always went slant-wise at his jumps : it's a capital plan. The horse gets his measure better ; he can give himself more room; if you put his head quite straight it's measured for him ; if you put him slantish, he measures it himself. . . .

He'd another dodge, when he rode at timber; *he always went slap at the post*; he said it made the horse fancy he'd more to do, and put more powder on. . . .

JACK-O'-LANTERN :

There used to be a sort of magic sympathy between the two, Mr. Smith, who always seemed to teach his horses to throw themselves sideways over their fences, would trot along, with the reins carelessly held in his left hand, and waving with his right to the hounds at a cast, and Jack would take him over fence after fence, as they came, such as would have stopped nine-tenths of a field in a run, while he never once seemed to take his eye off the hounds.—An instance of one of his diagonal leaps is thus recorded :

The hounds coming in the course of a run to an immensely high and steep bank, with a stile on the top of it, many gentlemen did not like its looks. Mr. Smith, throwing his whip into his left hand, and at the same time taking out his pocket handkerchief (this was done by way of giving the thing an air of negligence), said, " So you won't have it, Gentlemen ? " then taking the fence diagonally, he, by his peculiarly light hand, made his horse leap in this way, first on the bank, then over the stile and down on the other side. Nobody else could take the fence in the same manner, or would attempt it in any other. . . .

In some instances, with horses that he knew well he would ride for a fall, where he knew it was not possible for him to clear a fence. With Jack-o'-Lantern he was known often to venture on this experiment. " There is no place you cannot get over with a fall." To a young supporter of his pack, who was constantly falling and *hurting* himself, he said, " All who profess to ride should know *how to fall.*"

He determined to give Will his first lesson when he was little more than four stone. Putting him on one of his favourite hunters, he observed, by way of prelude, " Boy, if you don't stick close to me you'll never see your mother again ! " Having made this first and last appeal he proceeded to give him a lead over some hog-backed stiles, and chose one so close under a tree that the little fellow's hat was knocked off. In a minute his master was down picking it up. " Rare fun, this, boy, isn't it ? " " Yes, master," said young Hopeful, " but if we don't look sharp we won't see the hounds again ! " The retort suited his grim humour to a nicety, and he chuckled at the thoughts of it long after poor Will was in his grave.

Select is the circle in which I am moving,
  Yet open and free the admission to all ;
Still, still more select is that company proving,
  Weeded out by the funker and thinned by the fall ;
Yet here all are equal—no class legislation,
  No privilege hinders, no family pride :
In the " image of war " show the pluck of the nation ;
  Ride, ancient patrician ! democracy, ride !

BROMLEY DAVENPORT : *The Dream of an Old Meltonian.*

HOW TO RIDE AFTER *HOUNDS, AND TO DO THE THING WELL*

Take a sportsman, never mind his Dress, put him upon a decent Nag, and place him at the covert-side ; first goes away the Fox ; secondly goes away the body of the Hounds ; thirdly goes our Friend ; he steers straight as an arrow, observes the Hounds, and neither presses nor over-rides them ; keeping his horse together, does not blow him in ten minutes ; perseveres without any notion of jealousy at a certain rate, and with the pack, coming to a wood, enters a riding, and rides to the Cry ; goes away (as before) and especially notices the leading Dogs, and watches the conduct of all in any temporary difficulty ; as he was careful not to screech, interfere and spoil sport at the beginning, does the same towards the end of the run ; when the fox is killed, keeps his horse at a distance from the hounds, looks at his watch, calculates the whole extent of the ground gone over, as well as the length of the chase from point-to-point ; he talks over " the Thing," is overjoyed himself, and by civility and a display of old English character imparts Joy to all around him. If the Hounds try again, he stays for a second fox, and sees the whole of the Day.

Our said friend returns home at a gentle trot ; sits down with his family to a joint of meat and a pudding ; in a pint of Port, honest, genuine, old Port, toasts the Master of the Hounds, the King, the fair sex, fox-hunting and the unrivalled Nimrod of the age ; he retires to bed, wishing every Englishman to partake of public diversions suited to his taste, and fervently desiring, that the ancient reign of good humour, benevolence, hospitality etc., which marked the era of Sir Roger de Coverley, may speedily return.

The Flying Parson and Dick Christian : Edited by MAJOR GUY PAGET.

HOW TO RIDE OVER OR BEFORE *HOUNDS, AND TO DO THE THING ILL*

Take a youth of family, the more like a cinnamon tree the better, and allied (if possible) to a Knight of Malta ; examine his dress from top to toe, particularly the Cravat, and the appendages to breeches knees ; carry him five miles in a post chariot and four, and put him upon a long, lathy, thoroughbred Horse at the place of Meeting.

First goes away the fox, after having been three times headed ; secondly goes away two couple of hounds, and our Enemy ; thirdly goes the body of the Pack. The Hero of this tale steers straight I allow, but not like our friend ; having in the usual fit of jealousy gone along all abroad at the very outside of his pace, he choaks his steed, in ten minutes ; the Body now make their appearance, and he takes a second horse, scurries to catch them, and coming to a Wood cheers his allies, Fopling, Trippet, Lovelace, and Dandyprat, who pull up, give in and go home ; for a wonder our Enemy perseveres, follows the Huntsman through a riding, and goes away (as before) pressing, over-riding, and indifferent to the hounds, being anxious to lead the field, to go best, to gruel his horse, to ride over or before the hounds and to go at the Fox ; having exerted himself to spoil sport at the beginning, he does the same towards the end of the run, and when Reynard is killed rides into the middle of the hounds, and lames a favourite bitch ; in a soft, lisping, artificial, slow, tremulous voice asks "How long ?" Apparently divested of all feeling, he endeavours by reserve, formality, dullness, and a display of the opposite to the sterling old English character, to impart no Joy to his neighbours. Even if the hounds try again, he puts on a party-coloured Handerchief, takes two pinches of scented Snuff, and gallops home on a third hunter ; sits down to stewed meats, and Claret, gives an embellished report of his late proceedings in the field, arrogates to himself and his Allies the exclusive knowledge of the science of Hunting, the exclusive ability of riding to hounds, and, as he moves to bed, aristocratically threatens to petition Parliament, that no man not being a Member of either House, shall be permitted to join in the pursuit of the Fox.

The Flying Parson and Dick Christian : Edited by MAJOR GUY PAGET.

NIMROD: CHARLES JAMES APPERLEY

Charles James Apperley was born in 1777, the son of a Denbighshire country squire, but in 1822 owing to financial troubles he took to writing about horses, racing, and hunting chiefly, writing with zest and knowledge of the subject he loved. As special Foxhunting correspondent of the *Sporting Magazine* he received £1500 a year to maintain his stud of five hunters and a hack, with which he travelled the hunting countries of England, with visits to America and Europe. His writings contain a fund of anecdote as well as being of historical interest, due to his painstaking portrayal of all that he saw and the knowledge he possessed. He died in 1843. On Riding to Hounds he gives some advice in the following extract :—P. B.

Avoid deep ground as much as possible; but when in it keep a good pull on your horse, and by no means attempt to go so fast over it as you have been going over which was sound. Also avoid *crossing* fallows, or land sown with wheat. If obliged to go athwart them, get on the headland; or if you ride straight down them, choose the wettest furrow you can see. It is sure to have the firmest bottom, which is proved by the water standing in it. Next to a judicious choice of ground, is quickness in turning with hounds, as the difference between riding inside and outside of them in their turns (be it remembered hounds very seldom run straight) is very considerable indeed; and to a certain degree corresponds with what is called the "whip-hand" in a race. Never press upon hounds, even in chase. When they have lost the chase (in other words, when they are at fault), pull up your horse and keep wide of them, and, in the words of a celebrated old sportsman, "*always anticipate a check*"—but when your horse becomes distressed avoid timber, for if he do not clear it he will give you a worse fall in that state than if he were quite fresh. A blown horse falls nearly as heavy as a dead one.—A chief requisite to a good rider across country is courage, one of the most common qualities of human nature; and another is coolness.—The perfection of fine horsemanship in the hunting-field, then, is in a man riding well up to hounds, when going the best pace over a stiff country, and yet appearing to be quite at his ease, and his horse, as it were, sympathising with him in his calmness. Such a man (and there are some such in every hunt, but not many) is capable of taking every advantage that can be taken of country, hounds, and all obstacles which appear to oppose him in his career.—He is able to observe the beautiful working of the hounds, which is displayed to advantage with a burning scent; and he enjoys it the more in consequence of the superiority of his horsemanship having placed him in a situation where he is not molested by the crowd.—Nature is invariably the standard of excellence, and unless she have endowed you with a cool head, a vigorous body, and a stout heart, you will not long distinguish yourself in the hunting-field as what is now termed "*a first-flight horseman.*" You may sing with Hector.

"—*The foremost place* I claim,
The first in danger, as the first in fame;"

On a bad scenting day the wise man will give the huntsman a wide berth, thus saving himself from getting cursed and his horse from getting tired. On a good scenting day you may ride your horse up to seventy-five per cent. of his value.

LORD WILLOUGHBY DE BROKE: *Hunting the Fox.*

Boys, to the hunting-field ! though 'tis November,
The wind's in the south ;—but a word ere we start.—
Though keenly excited, I bid you remember
That hunting's a science, and riding an art.

R. E. EGERTON WARBURTON : From *A Word ere We Start.*

THE EXPERT

A LUCKY DAY, OR A HUNT WITH MR. X

Before we finally leave the subject of hunters we might have a hunt with, let us say, Mr. X, and see if we novices cannot pick up some useful hints from him. X is an artist on a young horse over a country, and at the same time he takes the most infinite pains in schooling, mouthing and balancing his horses.

On this occasion he is on a clean-bred five-year-old that he has hitherto been riding quietly out cub-hunting, but to-day he means to let him slip along in a hunt. Both rider and horse are immaculately turned out ; at the same time they look undeniably businesslike.

It chances to be one of those lucky days when everything goes right for X and his horse, but apart from any element of luck, much is due to the painstaking care he has bestowed on his pupil during the previous months.

On the morning in question the glass is rising steadily, the wind, slight as it is, has veered round to the north, and on the way to the Meet the fences, already cleaned by early November frosts, look black in the clear, calm atmosphere.

There should be a scent ?

Jogging quietly to the Meet, his horse the while playing with the bit in his mouth, X observes to himself, " Hounds will likely run to-day."

At the Meet it appears from their keen and alert expression that hounds have the same idea.

X allows his horse to walk quietly about, and on moving off, places himself behind the hunt second horseman. He is intent on letting his youngster have every chance and a good start, and is anxious to get into a position from which he can reconnoitre and prepare for it. He establishes himself at a gate outside

It appears from their keen and alert expression . . .

the small but thick thorn covert which hounds are drawing, and slightly on the down-wind side of it.

The Master holds up the rapidly increasing field at this point.

X's position is excellent should the fox go away on this side, and, by the chorus inside the covert, it seems that he has been right in his surmise of a scent, for hounds can really push their fox even in this dense black thorn. But their joyous music makes our friend's young horse restive, added to which he is alongside a fidgety and probable kicker, a not uncommon occurrence in a crowded field, but rather a trying situation when riding a high-mettled youngster. He has to make up his mind whether he shall stop where he is or move clear of the crowd now pressing round his horse.

He reasons that if the fox should break the other way he will not be too well placed, while every minute his horse is getting more eager and restive as he hears the cry of hounds in the covert. If he moves away and the fox breaks this side, he must jump the fence adjoining the gate. He should be able to do this even with horses going through the gate on his right, because he has always schooled his youngster to jump without wings and with others beside him. Can he rely on him now?

He decides to get clear of the crowd and selects his place in the fence, should he have to go that way. A momentary pause, then shrill through the cold air rings out Jack's, the first whipper-in's, "gone away" signal.

What commotion, cramming on of hats, snatching at bridles, as the huntsman comes galloping round and slips through the gate amidst cries of—"Huntsman, please, Huntsman——" Twang! twang! twang! sounds the horn, and hounds come streaming out of the covert.

X, clear of the turmoil, collects his horse and pops him over the fence, feeling justly elated that he never even thought of swerving towards the gate.

Striding over the grass, with the thud of galloping hoofs all round, the youngster shows all the natural symptoms of keenness and excitement only to be expected from his aristocratic breeding, but his perfect mouth and balance make it an easy matter for such a finished horseman to steady him.

What a wonderful sensation—a thoroughbred under one—that consciousness of power behind the saddle—that absolute smoothness of action, forelegs extended right out in front—a nice level feeling on the reins—the glorious rhythm of his paces over the sound springy turf—the rush of chill air against our face, as we gallop across a fifty-acre field.

So far all is plain sailing, and X steadies his horse as he approaches the next fence, a thorn hedge with a rail through it, but leaning away. He clears it just after the huntsman, landing well out in the next field.

" All on, sir," he hears Jack say to the huntsman, and all three settle down to ride alongside of the pack, which is running well and together across a big grass field.

X has got his start and is riding down wind of the pack about two hundred yards to the flank, just abreast of the last hounds. Each hound is racing and striving for mastery, and with a breast-high scent it will be a stout fox that can thwart them to-day.

The next fence, a stake and bound, is not such child's play, though luckily for X the ditch on the near side is clean ; nor is the fence too high, but the take-off slopes down towards the ditch. He steadies his horse almost to a trot, just keeps him collected so as not to lose the impulsion of his hind-legs, and they arrive in the next field safely and well—" Nicely off his hocks " is X's mental comment.

Hounds are now running well, over a country of mixed pasture and arable, fenced with low stiff hedges and occasional small flights of rails, but no ditches. They seem to be flying over the small fences like a covey of driven partridges skimming a low hedge. There is nothing to check the pace, and X's young horse, with his ears pricked, and an eye on the hounds racing on his flank, is near to paying the penalty of inexperienced youth.

After jumping a series of cock-fences, the next one, without any visible warning to rider and horse, has a wide ditch beyond. He stands back boldly, but it is just this boldness that is so near his undoing. The experienced hunter, having learnt his lesson, is always expecting a ditch on one side or the other of a fence ; if it is not on the take-off, he anticipates it on landing. Our youngster lands short in the ditch, which is shallow but heaped up with brambles. X gives him his head to have every chance of recovering, which he does with a snort and a scramble. " Well, it's a lesson to him, and the sooner learnt the better," mutters X to himself, and, no doubt, the prickly brambles scratching his thin silky skin bring the lesson home. X gives him a sympathetic pat on his neck to show that he does not really blame him, making due allowance for his anxiety to do the right thing.

After all the blunder was excusable. As is so often the case over small fences, competition had been keen. Each side and abreast of him horses were jumping, and a runaway bay, with his tongue over the bit, had just pulled across him.

X is most careful to ride up the furrows of the plough, and where the ridge and furrow on the grass is most pronounced, he turns down, when possible, to ride the headland along the fence.

It looks like being a real good thing, and it is vitally important to save every ounce of strength in a young horse. If he gets through this hunt without mishap he is practically a made hunter, five years old and yet a veteran.

We can now see X in absolute sympathy with his horse, standing up in his stirrups, just holding him together over a badly drained field, and gently curbing his impetuosity at the small fences. A blood-horse has a tendency to jump in " chasing form " : that comes naturally to him, and X, realising the fact, seems bent on making him jump collectedly and arch his back over his fences. He has done it at home, and he is settling down now and fencing in the finished style of a perfect hunter with absolute freedom, yet collecting himself and jumping off his hocks each time.

X has just landed over some broken rails with a ditch beyond, at which he has allowed his horse to slip along and spread himself well over, when he sees, what he knew he would have to face sooner or later, a blind ditch in front of a rather formidable-looking fence. Quick as lightning he selects the weakest-looking place, but the take-off here as elsewhere is undefined. He steadies first to a canter, then to a trot, and keeping his legs to his horse and the lightest contact with his mouth, he presents him at the fence. The youngster recognises his master's aids and appears to realise that some special effort is required of him. He lowers his head, hesitates for a fraction of a second as to whether he should put in another short stride, when he feels his rider's legs vigorously applied behind his girths, then jumps, and jumps well enough to give X a sensation of intense satisfaction, not to say relief.

The understanding was evidently mutual. It looked as if the horse had just felt the ditch, a very blind one, with one fore-leg but not with both. But his hocks were well placed ready to jump, when the question was asked, and thus save a fall. At the pace hounds are running a fall would have meant irretrievable disaster, whereas this achievement definitely confirms our friend's opinion of the pace and manner to ride at a really blind place.

Hounds are now racing uphill, and the pace is beginning to tell even on a fit blood-horse. To X's relief, he perceives a herd of cattle in the next field, and he also sees the leading hounds beginning to check. Quickly and quietly he pulls up his horse and allows him to stand with his head to the wind. But the respite is only too short.

Two couple of hounds are feathering along the fence in the corner of the field ; first Rapid, then Melody, throw their tongues, when they are immediately joined by the rest of the pack, and with noses to the ground they carry the line through the fence, right-handed down the road, and then through a gap into the field on the far side. X, who is handy to the gate, unhitching the latch on the right with his whip in his left hand, holds it open for the huntsman, then quietly follows him out on to the road and over the fence on the far side. As he does so he sees a horse and rider slip up on the road on his right. Both are on their legs again, but the pace is too good to inquire further. With one eye on hounds, X instinctively selects his place in the fence on the far side of the field. At the same time a lesson learnt in boyhood crosses his mind : namely, when you jump into a road, intending to turn on landing, or if other people are riding down it, always jump the fence at an angle, or your horse will most probably slip up when turning sharply on the road : with the modern tarmac road it is a practical certainty.

Hounds industriously work out the line over the next three fields, which carry a bad scent, having been recently dressed with chemical manure. Some of the field, pressing on hounds, are severely censured by the Master, but X holds back and is content to keep pretty wide on the down-wind side of the pack.

By degrees there is more assurance in the cry of the leading hounds, then all join in the chorus as they carry the line in and out of a grass lane, part of the famous old Roman road that stretches straight across the country. The next moment they can be seen in the field on the far side racing away from us with tremendous drive. There is no time to lose, yet without any apparent hurry X jumps very deliberately in and out of the lane. He holds his horse straight at the fence into the road and lands on the grass. He is ready to check instantly any tendency to turn down the road, and using his legs firmly, keeps his youngster both collected and straight up to the fence out of it : then gives him the office and leans slightly forward. The horse jumps without hesitation, and lands clean over the ditch and fence into the opposite field.

The line of pollards now in sight clearly indicates a well-known brook, and there is no bridge within a mile. But by this stage of the hunt both rider and horse have complete confidence in one another. It will not be the fault of either if this formidable obstacle is not successfully negotiated. Hounds are in and scrambling up the opposite bank. X wisely selects his place where there is a bush growing on the bank and probably a sound take-off. Between forty and fifty yards from the brook he steadies his horse, and does not attempt to put on steam till he is about fifteen yards from the near bank. There is thus less chance of his misjudging the take off, and in fact they clear it by three feet, the glint of blue water flashing under them as they sail through the air.

As X looks round he sees the numbers of his companions considerably reduced ; the brook apparently has taken its toll of some less fortunate sportsmen—" Nothing like blood when it comes to spreading themselves," he remarks to himself.

But the very next fence is almost his undoing. It is thick and impenetrable, with, probably, a ditch beyond, and he presents his horse at it with his accustomed skill and care. He first pulls him together about twenty yards from the fence to ensure having his hocks well under him, then lets him go, just giving him a squeeze with his legs as he takes off. In mid-air he realises that there is a big drop and possibly a sticky landing too. That they did not fall was probably due to X's quick adjustment of his seat, as well as to his horse's grandly sloping shoulders. He leans well back and lets the reins slip through his fingers. If the horse is to save himself he will want all the freedom of his head that he can get. He does peck, and his nose and one knee meet the wet ground. But he has that spare leg of the clever fencer and liberty to use it too. Having got him on his legs again, X just nurses him and holds him together over the heavy going. Hounds swing left-handed towards him, and, easing up, he turns with them and jumps the next fence out of a trot. Perhaps it was a mistake in this instance, as there is a much wider ditch on the landing side than he reckoned with. He probably misled his horse, seeing that it has been his wont to urge him on with more speed when it was obviously necessary to spread himself. But here again good shoulders and a proper use of them saves a fall. In mid-air X feels his horse make an effort to extend his fore-legs to the utmost, so that, at any rate, they shall clear the ditch, while he himself leans forward in his saddle so as not to hamper his horse's loins and quarters unnecessarily, should they drop short. All is well : there is just a bit of a scramble, and, no doubt, if he had not kept his weight forward, both rider and horse would have slipped back in the ditch.

Hounds hunt their fox on through Bingley Wood, and X trots down the centre ride. He feels sure they are close on their quarry and dares not lose sight of them, as he knows the earths here are stopped. But he does not gallop up the middle of the holding ride ; he hugs his horse as it were, keeping on the side that appears to be the soundest going, holding him together, conserving all possible energy and retaining up his sleeve, as it turns out, enough " go " to enable him to continue to the end.

Clear of the wood we are out of our country, and our stout fox appears to be heading for the Lime Kyln Hangings. X sees a man waving his hat, and wishing to save his horse, canters across the sound turf of Slangton Park in that direction, thus cutting off the arc that hounds are running round the

He is a stout old customer who has baffled hounds more than once before.

home-farm. The man calls out that the fox is just ahead, very muddy and tired, and that it ran through a sheep-soiled pasture, where hounds have just thrown up. X watches them make their own cast. First Rhapsody owns it, and, confirmed by old Energy's glorious note, the whole pack drive on. He will indeed be a lucky fox if he reaches the Hangings before hounds catch him.

Nevertheless he does. He is a stout old customer that has baffled hounds more than once before. But a bitch pack like this hunts for hunting's sake, and though they richly deserve their fox, they are, should they lose him, if possible, even more eager to catch him next time.

Ere they reach the Hangings there are two further incidents that add to the stock of knowledge in the education of our friend's young horse. Hounds were not expected in these parts to-day, and the huntsman and X ride up to a gate only to find it locked. There is no jumpable place in the fence and hounds are running on, now a field ahead.

The huntsman rides at the gate, but there is a nasty poached take-off and his horse refuses. Though they can hear their cry they can no longer see hounds, who are over the fence beyond, and if one may judge by the crows hovering above indicating his course, their quarry is not far ahead of them.

"Can you give us a lead, sir?" exclaims the huntsman. X, who is twenty yards from the gate, presses his horse up to his bit, comes up to the gate at a collected canter and just "gives to" his horse's mouth as he lowers his head, still pressing him with his legs. Both are now conscious that they are placed just right to take off, and, to confirm this, X again closes his legs, leaning forward as his horse rises, and giving him the rein he requires as he lands. Nothing could be better, and the assurance with which the youngster clears the gate is apparently conveyed to the huntsman's horse, who is soon following in his wake.

The country hounds are now running over is bullock grazing land, well-drained pastures, but with big ugly fences to meet at the end of a hunt.

X makes up his mind that it will be foolish to try his horse too high at this juncture, and keeps an eye for handy gates to use if necessary. Just on his right the Master takes on an undefined-looking fence, but it is the only place that looks jumpable and X is prepared to follow him. It turns out to be a biggish bottom, a boundary fence between adjoining estates. Our Master is down, but clear of his horse as he rolls over on his side. X pulls up—"Are you all right, Master?" he shouts. "Yes thanks, but it's a nasty place," comes back the answer, and X with good judgement canters across to a gate, even though it is a bit out of his line. He then trots down a grass lane—no sign of hounds. He pulls up to listen—all is silent. Hullo, that sounds like the horn ! No, it is only a bullock lowing in a distant field. His horse impatiently paws the ground, and X gives a shake of his bridle to keep him quiet, the more easily to catch any possible sound or signal. Is that a holloa ? No, a train engine whistling. What tricks one's imagination plays ! X suspects the fox has been headed by the man with the team of horses hauling timber from the wood and turned right-handed. Then he observes a blackbird fly screeching out of the fence running at right angles to the lane. Later the deep note of a hound electrifies him and his horse, and the pack, still invisible, immediately joins in the chorus. Next instant the dry brittle fence vibrates and bends with their weight as with increased melody the whole pack bursts into the adjoining field, each hound striving and racing for mastery. Imagine X's delight as he spots first Mermaid, then Modesty, leading, two of last year's entry that he had walked as puppies.

He is now joined by the huntsman cheering them on, and together they canter down the grass lane.

Unfortunately, before they have gone very far, the line that our fox has taken diverges from the lane. X pulls up at a gap on his right. It is not too nice a place, as it necessitates first sliding down a precipitous embankment, then popping over a ditch at the bottom into the same field as hounds. He makes his horse walk through the gap, then slide down the grassy slope on his hind-legs. As long as he keeps him straight they cannot fall, and to ensure doing this he holds his horse's forehand straight with the reins, and his hind-quarters well under control with his legs. There are two long parallel tracks cut deep in the turf by his horse's hind shoes. Just as he approaches the ditch at the bottom he gives his horse a vigorous squeeze with his legs, and together they land in the field, just in time to catch a glimpse of the tail hounds entering the wood and making the welkin ring with their chorus.

GEOFFREY BROOKE : *Horse-Sense and Horsemanship of To-day.*

A RETROSPECT

Although the flickering twilight of life may be stealing upon us, and we can no longer follow the chase, let us not repine, but rather revert with pleasure to the rapturous joys which in bygone days it has afforded us : how, in glancing over the pack, we have been gratified by the shining coat, the sparkling eye—

sure symptoms of fitness for the fight ;—how, when thrown in, every hound has been hidden ; how every sprig of gorse has bristled with motion ; how when viewed away by the sharp-eyed whipper-in, he stole under the hedge ; how the huntsman clapped round, and with a few toots of his horn brought them out in a body ; how without tying on the line, they flew to head ; how, when they got hold of it, they drove it, and, with their heads up, felt the scent on both sides of the fence ; how with hardly a whimper, they turned with him, till at the end of fifty minutes they threw up ; how the patient huntsman stood still ; how they made their own cast ; and how, when they came back on his line, their tongues doubled and they marked him for their own. As the old woman in the fable regaled her nostrils with the redolence of the dregs of the Falernian wine, so does the old sportsman cheer his flagging spirits by recalling to his mind the days when youth, and strength, and buoyancy gave zest to the delights of the chase.

THE DRUID : *Silk and Scarlet*, 1859.

Deprive him of horses and hounds as you will,
A fox-hunter once is a fox-hunter still.

RACE RIDING

THE resolute canter down the straight,
The eager line at the starting-gate,
The barrier lifted when side by side;
A dozen racers leap into their stride.

WILL. H. OGILVIE: *Saddles Again.*

Those who have only seen race-horses on a race-course would be surprised to witness what diminutive urchins ride many of them in their training, and the perfect command they obtain over them. . . . Considering the prodigious number of race-horses in training, and that each horse has its lad, it is astonishing that more accidents do not occur. As we have before observed, almost all race-horses are playful ; and " horseplay is rough," but we do not wonder at their becoming vicious ; highly bred as they are, hot in blood, and their tender and nearly hairless skins irritated by a coarse brush, and, after sweating, scraped with rather a sharp wooden instrument,—that, we repeat, is no wonder. Nevertheless, it seldom happens that they hurt the boys who look after them. Indeed, it is an interesting sight to witness a little urchin of a stable-boy approach, with perfect safety to himself, an animal that would perhaps be the death of the strongest man in the land who might be rash enough to place himself within his reach. To what shall we attribute this passive obedience of an animal of such vast power and proud spirit to a diminutive member of the creation—an abortion of nature, indeed, as we might be almost induced to call him—Whether to self-interest or to gratitude, to love or to fear, or to that unspeakable magic power which the Almighty has given to the eye and voice of even the child of man ?

NIMROD : *The Turf*, 1852.

A morning with John Scott the famous jockey and trainer of old, on Langton Wold in the words of " The Druid," 1862 :

Baron Alderson only wrote half of his recollections of his visit. He might have told how he questioned Frank, on the whole art of riding ; how wondered not so much at the condition of the horses as where the supply of boys came from, and the solution of the difficulty ; how he noted down, at Jim Perren's dictation, some of their most remarkable titles, " Spider," " Cudjoe," " Frog," " Weasel," " Squeaky," etc.

The scene on Langton Wold :

Cape Flyaway, as true a trier as Dilkoosh or Backbiter, leads Sweetsauce, who, in his white quarter piece, and with Jack Charlton up, comes striding along as if the Goodwood Cup field were at his heels once more. The next are a lot of Barbatuses, and the Miss Whip colt ; and the Wizard comes up, nearly pulling double over his schoolmaster, the ever bold Benbow. Then the green furze at the distance is suddenly alive with sterns, and the word is passed :—" There are Morgan and the hounds " coming over the wold from Birdsall. Ben draws them up on a little knoll, and John Scott gets out of his phaeton to give them greeting, and beckons Jim Perren to bring up the horses, and " let them walk near us in a ring."—" Don't take off too much at once, Jim, from The Drone." " Now you may go home with Sweetsauce, you've done enough for this morning," " Walk Longrange, and bring him steadily along a mile ; mind keep your hands down, Ginger ! " " Jack just get up again and lead him ! " float to us occasionally, as John, with his adjutant, scans each of the troop.

Now the council is over, and he turns once more to the hounds.

Speaking very broadly, it may be said that the two chief essentials for a jockey are head and hands ; the former is a very comprehensive term implying many qualities inherent and acquired, the latter is almost entirely a natural gift.

. . . .

It happened one day that a match was to be ridden at Newmarket with Archer and Tom Cannon in the saddle, and Fordham was looking on. The match was a very good one, that is to say, both horses were fit and well, and on form there was nothing to choose between them ; they started and raced together side by side, and Fordham watched as the pair approached the place where he stood, not far from the winning post. " Sit still, Tom, my boy ; sit still " ; a friend who stood by him heard him mutter to himself in a low tone that was just audible. " Sit still—that's it ! that's it ! No ! not just yet—sit still—not yet ! No—steady—Now ! Now ! Now ! " The " Now ! " came out with startling suddenness, Fordham bringing his right fist into his left palm as he cried out ; and at the precise moment that he uttered the syllable, Cannon, who had been waiting with the utmost patience, made his effort, and by a vigorous piece of riding got his horse past the post a short head in front of the other. . . .

The striking part of this little story consists in the fact that to Fordham, standing by the rails and watching with the keen and critical eye of an unrivalled expert, and to Cannon on the horse's back, it was equally evident when, to the tick of a second, the effort had to be made ; and no one who has any acquaintance with the niceties of the art can need to be told that if that second had been missed or anticipated the race would have been lost instead of won.

FRED ARCHER :

He was riding a very speedy but uncertain animal called Southampton, in a field of eleven starters. Scarcely more than half of the distance had been covered, when Archer leaned forward and patted his horse's neck. He had won his race, the famous jockey remarked afterwards when some casual comment was made on his action, and it struck the writer as a wonderful thing that while yet so far from the post, in the dash and turmoil of the struggle, one look round should have revealed the whole state of the race and enable Archer to see that he was safe.

An old trainer of wide knowledge and experience had a horse in a handicap with a very light weight. The little lad who was to ride emerged from the weighing room in colours, with a big whip in his hand and a pair of well-polished spurs on his small boots ; and the trainer regarded him critically. . . . " I don't think I should ride him with spurs," he thoughtfully remarked. " N–o, my boy, I think you'd better take them off perhaps."

The lad glanced down at his boots rather regretfully, but of course turned round, re-entered the room, and soon appeared with unarmed heels.

" Yes, that's better ; I'm sure that's much better," the trainer observed encouragingly. " Now give me your whip, and you'll do capitally." The boy, with a very reluctant look at it, handed up his whip. He had perhaps pictured himself riding a desperate finish and just beating Archer a short head amid the admiring cheers of the crowd ; but there was nothing for it but obedience ; he was put up, rode his horse home manfully with his hands, and did in fact win a race in which with whip and spurs he would very likely have been beaten.

ALFRED E. T. WATSON : *Race Riding*, Badminton Library, 1891.

Prior to the opening of the season 1884 *The Illustrated Sporting and Dramatic News* published an interesting interview with Fred Archer of which the following are extracts :—

When asked the secret of success, Archer replied with a smile : " Well, I really don't quite know. I never throw away a chance in a race if I can help it, and am always looking out to see how I can steal a length or two by getting the rails or anything of that sort, and then I generally manage to get well away. But what people say, and what I sometimes read in some of the papers about the starter favouring Archer, and his being off a couple of lengths to the good, is not true. In fact it's rubbish.

" Of course, I don't mean to say that I don't do my best to get away when the flag falls, but it isn't the getting away first so much as how you get away—how you set your horse going. I mean, that makes all the difference. You can't set a horse going at once if you have a tight hold of his head. You often see a jockey at the post in a five-furlong race pulling at his horse, as nervous as he can be, watching the starter. The flag falls, and he lets go of the reins, ready to start off at his best pace. I've always got my horse ready to go, but not pulling at him, and then when we do start I'm off at full speed at once. If you watch you'll often see that some jockey was off a couple of lengths before me, but if his horse wasn't ready he doesn't keep his advantage."

The interviewer suggested to Archer that he was not as severe on horses as he used to be. " You're quite right," he frankly replied. " It's a great mistake to knock a horse about, and I know that a few years back I was a severe rider. I've learnt better by experience. I rarely hit a horse more than twice in a finish now, and I rarely or never have rowels to my spurs. You can hurt a horse almost as much without, for the matter of that, if you want to, but it's bad policy to hurt them."

JOCKEYSHIP :

It is often said that a certain horse goes better for a particular jockey. In my experience this is only a half-truth. There may be isolated cases, but, generally speaking, it is the jockey's style of riding which suits the horse best, rather than the jockey himself—The ideal jockey is obviously the one who can ride equally well on any horse.—Through the race is where I think jockeyship really counts as compared to the much-talked-of strength or weakness of different jockeys in a finish. Comparisons are odious, and praise or blame of a jockey from one of his own kidney must be equally so, and I will refrain from either except to say that in my opinion, Danny Maher was the best combination of both I have known. He may have lost a race through making his run too late, but I never saw him win a race and lose it again, however near or far from home. His method, as a rule, of waiting till the very last second he could got him into tangles, sometimes, but as an all-rounder he was a very fine rider indeed, and even if I consider him the best, I have had the pleasure of riding with several others who have run him very close, in spite of what people say to the contrary. Maher was as near perfection, I think, as is humanly possible. He had the gift of beautiful hands, a good seat, could adapt his style to any type of horse—vigour when it was needed, yet the patience of Job !—perfect judgement of pace, always knew exactly where the winning post was, and, what perhaps is the greatest essential of the lot, a very cool and level head. . . .

An over-free horse seldom stays. It is said of them that when " they have done pulling they have done going," and a lot of this is attributable to excessive livening-up in their early days. The best stayers are behind their bridles, or only just up to them, never pullers. Lots of horses would stay, that otherwise do not, if bred at all that way and are ridden patiently and quietly, and taught to what is called " settle down " in a race—that is, be content to be behind without pulling. A jockey may be able to hold a horse behind by force, but it doesn't make him stay any better, because he is using up a lot of energy by pulling and so has nothing left in reserve. To teach a horse to settle down is another case where horsemanship comes in, especially hands. The gift of " hands " on a horse is a thing very difficult to explain, but it makes all the difference. A light boy with good hands can hold a horse that would run away with a boy much heavier and with twice his physical strength, and a lot of happiness or unhappiness of the horse depends on the good or bad hands of his rider. A well-known trainer in my hearing once told a boy, whose hands were a bit rough and heavy, that " he had bad hands," and the boy said he couldn't think he had because they never " hurt him a bit " ! The horse's mouth should be a great consideration, of course, as it is the principal, and often the only, link between the horse and his rider, especially as regards race-horses in these days of the American seat. In " high school " riding and polo the legs play a big part, but the horse itself must be taught to correspond to them, and the rider with only about a foot or eighteen inches of stirrup leather cannot do much in that line anyway. Judgement of pace has not the same significance at Epsom as on a lot of courses—that is decided for you by the others ! This term needs a little explanation, as it has a far different meaning to a jockey than to the man in the street. To the latter, pace means so many miles an hour or part of an hour. Even our Gordon Richards estimated the speed of his car at thirty, but the policeman's watch said forty, so he won ! To a jockey on a horse it means, in short, getting through the race in the best time in which the particular horse he is riding is capable of travelling the whole distance, or varying his pace at different stages to suit the horse, so that he does not tire before the end, and, as far as possible, to the disadvantage of his opponents. To a horse that stays really well, a good pace, or what is called a level gallop, is essential, having regard to the stamina and turn of speed of the others, while to one whose speed, rather than stamina, is his strong point, on the pace at which the race is run in the early part will depend his chance of winning. A paradoxical part of this is—time taken for a race does not necessarily mean it was fast or slowly run.

Judgement of pace also plays a big part on the training grounds, and ability to do this well both there and on the race-course is one of the chief assets of a jockey. I never saw Tod Sloan ride, but have been told that he could do this to perfection. A moderate horse can go with a good one for at least some of the journey, and in a falsely run race the best horse is not always sure to win. I was fooled this way a time or two in Germany, where the straight is not nearly so long on many courses as it is here. I had waited behind, in a slowly run race, till we got into the straight, and the leaders sprinted home and I hadn't time to catch 'em ! I soon learned better, though, and when I was riding a good favourite, which often happened, if no one went along I went myself. That is judgement of pace !

A good horseman doesn't ask his horse to improve into his best pace by *loosening* the reins, he would be more apt to sprawl, but by taking a shorter and tighter hold—what we call "picking him up." When riding a hard puller in half-speed exercise work this should be remembered, and the rider should take one good hold at the start and not move his hands afterwards. Let him do this and try to get a fresh hold, he will be sorry nine times out of ten, because the horse will pull up when he's tired, not when the rider wishes ! Another phase of a jockey's life and work is the advice and help he is, or should be, able to give the trainer.

Several trainers whose knowledge has been acquired by years of experience and practice have told me that a jockey, named Jim Snowden, who rode mostly in the North, was the best judge among jockeys they ever knew, and was as near infallibility as possible. They say he could ride a horse in a race, and then tell them what race, what distance, and on what course to run him, and even approximately what weight he would get down to before they could back him to win it !

To get to this standard of efficiency must be an education in itself ; or is it a gift ? Anyway it is only one of the things that a jockey should know.

F. Fox : "Jockeyship," *Flat Racing*, Lonsdale Library.

STEEPLECHASING

. . . Choice of the heart's desire,
A short life in the saddle, Lord!
Not long life by the fire.
Louise Imogen Gurney.

QUALIFICATIONS FOR STEEPLECHASE RIDER

These are exactly what are wanted in a very fast run over a stiffly enclosed country with fox-hounds ; namely, a fine bridle-hand, a steady seat, a cool head, undaunted courage, and above all things, great quickness, and very prompt decision. But the steeplechase jockey has one evil to guard against, which the racing jockey is, comparatively, but little subject to, and this is a fall. The best preventive of it is keeping a horse well together, and making him go in a collected form at his fences, as well as over rough ground. But, at the same time, he must not overpace his horse, or he will not be able to rise at his fences when he gets to them. And here lies the great difficulty after all, as far as the horse is concerned. He must go, at least he is called upon to go at a much quicker rate than he can reasonably be expected to maintain for any considerable length of time, without becoming distressed, because his competitors in the race are also doing so, and he will be left behind to a certainty, if his rider do not endeavour to make him keep with them.

That horse, then, has the best chance to win which, barring a fall, is the stoutest runner and surest fencer, and whose rider is good enough, and strong enough, to give him all the assistance he requires, at least as much as a rider can give him, to enable him to struggle through his difficulties to the end. But there is one quality in a horse, especially calculated for steeplechase racing, and that is *quickness*. After fencing, some are on their legs again, and get away instantly, as soon as they alight on the ground, be the fence ever so large; whilst others dwell for some time after landing, previously to their recovering their equilibrium, and so lose time. It is evident, then, that a quick horse with a quick man on his back, is best adapted to a steeplechase.

NIMROD: *The Horse and the Hound,* 1832.

The ladies wave their kerchiefs as the rival jumpers start,
A smile of such encouragement might nerve the faintest heart.

THE FIRST GRAND NATIONAL

This was run on 26th Feb. 1839 being called the Grand Liverpool steeplechase. A sweepstake of 20 sovs. each, 5 sovs. forfeit, with 100 sovs. added. There were seventeen runners including three entries from Ireland, owned by Harkaway Ferguson, the leading Irish owner: Daxon, Barkston, and Rust, the first being ridden by his owner and the most fancied. Owing to the number of runners—from the first, to be one of the features of the race (in Gregalach's year, 1929, there was a field of 66 runners)—it took some time before all the jockeys were weighed out at 12 stone, and the race started two hours late. Lottery ridden by Jem Mason was favourite at 5–1. His owner, John Elmore, the dealer, had bought the horse three years previously at Horncastle fair for £120 and handed him over to Jem Mason to school. Mason got him so handy that he could jump him over garden chairs, and a table set for a meal. Lord Sefton, the starter, eventually got the field away and the roar of "They're off!" rolled across Aintree's ploughs for the first time in this the forerunner of the greatest steeplechase in the world. It would seem that even the first race was full of thrills and excitement. All the hazards and fates were at work to test the courage and endurance of man and horse. Daxon had several lengths lead over the first fence, strong-growing hawthorn with a stout guard rail, the first of 29 jumps. Fifteen on the first circuit, and fourteen on the second, nearly all natural, strong-growing fences and added to to make them more formidable, including a specially built wall nearly 5 feet high in front of the stand. Daxon comes back to his field over the heavy plough but Captain Becher on Conrad is moving up to him, and the pair go into the next fence almost together ; this is a stream that has been dammed up to make it 8 feet of running water. Standing 3 feet back from the brook on the take-off side is a strong timber fence, 3½ feet high, which stands in heavy plough and is a good 3 feet higher than the next field. Daxon hits the top rail and is nearly down, Conrad breasts the rails and shoots Captain Becher head first into the brook, where he ducks down as Lottery, Rust, The Nun, Dictator, Charity and the rest of the field jump over him. Then out he jumps and with water pouring off him, and squelching in his boots runs across the next field, catches his horse, and has caught up with his field again as they are slowed by plough and sticky wheat fields. Little did he know then of the immortal fame that he had achieved by his fall—" Becher's Brook " to this day. Conrad and his redoubtable rider are actually with the leaders again, but at the next fence, another rail and brook, but followed by a sharp left-hand turn in front of the canal, Conrad's effort has been too much for him and down he comes with several others ; this time the gallant Captain's efforts to catch his horse are unavailing. The race goes on without him, round to the big wall 4′ 8″ high in front of the stand where Charity falls. Rust is also out of the race, trapped in a lane, where the yokels block his exit. Daxon still leads going away on the second circuit, with Lottery moving up to him, Dictator, True Blue, Paulina, The Nun, Seventy Four ridden by Tom Oliver, Pioneer, and Railroad are still standing. At the next fence Dictator falls dead, then Daxon is down, and the Nun falls at the rails and ditch after the turn in front of the canal. Lottery is in front now, and jumping beautifully, Seventy Four is moving up, but cannot make any impression on the leader, and Lottery wins the first Grand National in a canter, from Seventy Four, Paulina, True Blue, Railroad, and Pioneer.

It must be remembered too, that the course lay over a natural country, deep plough, ridge and furrow, low ground where the rain lay, cart-rutted tracks, and muddy gateways—no made-up sloped fences with sound take-offs in a railed course of thick growing old turf. Four miles from start to finish but it must have been nearer five as galloped by those great-hearted horses and gallant riders who finished the race.—P. B.

"Becher's Brook" to this day.

John Elmore was the best of companions, and had a good story to tell of every horse or sporting man that could be named. One of Carlin, the steeplechase jockey, especially delighted him. " Where have you been to ? " he said when that worthy did not arrive until some minutes after the ruck. " You told me to leave it all to the horse, and I trusted to his honour, and he put me down—that's a pretty thing." After Lottery had been retired, having defied creation by winning with Jem Mason, carrying thirteen stone seven, and whenever friends of Elmore's went down to see him, he would have the old horse saddled. " Hang it ! " he would say. " Have you never been on the old horse ?—get up ! " and however hard the ground or blind the fences, he would insist on their getting up on him, one after another if there were several of them. For lack of a handier fence he would put them over the iron railings between the garden and the paddock, or he would put the rustic chairs together.

THE TWO GREATEST STEEPLECHASES IN THE WORLD COMPARED

The Maryland Hunt Cup and the Grand National at Aintree are associated in people's minds as the greatest steeplechases of America and England, but though each is run over a very stiff country, they are different in many respects. I will try to tell you a few of the differences, and perhaps you will realise why they are so difficult to win.

The Grand National Steeplechase is run over a beautiful flat turf course, twice round, a total distance of four and one-half miles, over thirty big brush fences all in the vicinity of five feet. The fences have the most perfect take-offs imaginable because the ground, several strides away, is graded up to meet the fence. This incline is very slight, but undoubtedly it is a tremendous help to horses racing into such big fences at such a fast clip. Several fences have a very noticeable drop on the landing side which is greatly increased by the graded take-off. A horse jumping in good form, however, will land out far enough not to be bothered by the drops. Only when a horse gets in wrong and has to put in a short one will he fall or peck, as then he lands too close to the fence, off balance.

All the fences of the Grand National are either growing hedges or birch compressed in a frame, the whole thing covered with green pine or cedar, which in turn is neatly cut and trimmed so that the top edges of the fences are rounded off. They are all straight up and down, and very wide, but are the best constructed and most neatly built fences I have ever seen. There is a certain amount of give to the top of the fences, which enables a tired horse to slide over a few without falling, if he is lucky enough to get his knees over.

The class of horse that runs in the National now is the best, since the new restrictions for qualifying are so severe that nothing but a really good class 'chaser can start. The majority of the National field are comparable to the stake horses over here that run in steeplechases at Belmont, Saratoga, Laurel, and Pimlico—horses like Green Cheese, Chenango, Arc Light, Tourist II, and Beacon Hill. They seldom race in anything but a really rich stake and then the competition is very keen. Where would your timber horse or hunt meeting horse be in a race against the few horses mentioned above? Absolutely no place.

A National horse must be a good, bold jumper, but he must also have a lot of class, speed and staying power, otherwise he won't have much chance of getting around, much less winning a truly run National. Of course, the enormous number of starters adds to the uncertainty of the race, particularly when the going is bad and there is so much interference from loose and fallen horses.

This year the National was a truly run horse race, but not a typical National. By this I mean that there was practically no interference from loose or refusing horses, as is usually the case, and every horse had a fair chance. They all ran and jumped straight until they tired, when they dropped back instead of running across the field.

The new conditions will help greatly to make the National a better horse race and the size of the purse will attract every eligible. Further, the fact that this race stands supreme in the steeplechasing world makes it the ambition of everyone to win.

Incidentally, the National is one of many races at a big three-day meeting run like the meetings at Laurel or Pimlico. There are parimutuel betting, hundreds of book-makers, admission charges, regular grand-stands and enclosures, and a card of six or seven races consisting of flat races, hurdle races and steeplechases over part of the National course.

The Maryland Hunt Cup, America's great event, on the other hand, is the only race at its meeting. It is run over a natural hunting country, a very rolling up-and-down-hill course, although the grades are not steep. There is no admission charge and no grand-stand except a natural hill above the paddock from which practically every part of the race can be seen comfortably. The Maryland Hunt Cup is four miles, a half mile shorter than the Grand National.

A mistake in the Maryland is fatal.

The fences, twenty-two in number, are all timber, ranging in height from three feet nine inches to five feet. They are all stiff, straight up and down, with a lot of daylight showing through them. Due to the rolling country, the fences are jumped uphill, downhill, on the side of a hill, out of old roadways; some even appear to lean toward the horses and their riders, which is very different from the perfect National take-offs.

A Maryland Hunt Cup horse must be primarily a brilliant and phenomenal jumper, because unless he can jump fences with such irregular take-offs and measure them with uncanny accuracy, he can't possibly complete the course. Very few do. A mistake in the Maryland is fatal, as seldom does a rail break.

The highest class horse in the world could not win the Maryland Hunt Cup unless he was an extraordinary jumper, able to take off perfectly and arc over his fences, although he might jump every brush course in the world well, including the Grand National. The really brilliant jumper with no claim to class or real speed has a good chance in the Maryland.

Another marked difference between the two races is the number of starters, the Maryland having usually about one-third as many as the Grand National. Consequently there is little or no interference at all in the Maryland. The fact that the pace is much slower may have a great deal to do with this, as horses are more in hand.

The Maryland Hunt Cup, unlike the National, is for amateur riders only and has no money value, the race being run for a silver tankard and the Whistler Challenge Cup.

I think the Maryland Hunt Cup is much the more difficult course to jump, due to the type of fence and the irregularity of the take-offs, but that the Grand National is the more difficult race to win, because the class of horse is so good, the fields are so large, and the pace is so fast that many good horses come to grief through no fault of their own.

I rode Mrs. T. H. Somerville's Trouble Maker in both races and he was equally fit and well in each of them. The weather and the going were identical: a cool, clear day, with wonderful, firm turf to race over.

In the Maryland Hunt Cup, Trouble Maker was in front for the first mile and not setting much pace either, then he was passed by two horses, and ran third for about another mile. He was second starting the fourth mile and gradually moved up on the leader, winning by a head, after sprinting to Brose Hover in the stretch.

In the Grand National, we did not get off too well from the start, but the old horse was galloping at a very fast pace all the way, yet he could not improve his position. Everything in the race seemed to be flying. There was no

Everything in the race seemed to be flying.

rating or taking back at fences so far as I could see. Then when the pace-makers dropped out of it, about a mile from home, eight or ten horses just behind them sprang into the lead and raced as hard as they could for home. It took a super-horse to be in that forward group at the finish.

There is as much difference in pace between the Grand National and the Maryland Hunt Cup as there is between a good average timber race, and a short, fast brush race over here.

In conclusion, I will say that I would look forward with the greatest pleasure to another ride at Aintree, but shudder at the thought of riding in the Maryland Hunt Cup again.

NOEL LAING : *Polo Magazine*, Oct. 1933.

A FIRST RIDE IN A POINT-TO-POINT

Mr. Gaffikin then tied the strings of my cap in a very tight bow ; a bell jangled and a stentorian voice shouted, " Now then gentlemen, I'm going down to the post." The blue sky suddenly went white ; my heart bumped ; I felt dazed and breathless. Then Mr. Gaffikin's remote voice said, " Let me give you a leg up, old chap " ; I grabbed hold of the reins, lifted an awkward foot, and was lifted airily on to the slippery saddle : Cockbird gave one prance and then stood still ; Dixon was holding him firmly by the head. Pressing my knees into the saddle I overheard Mr. Gaffikin's ultimate advice. " Don't go in front unless you can help it ; but *keep well with 'em*." They both wished me luck and released me to my destiny. I felt as if I'd never been on Cockbird's back before ; everything around me appeared unreal and disconnected from all my previous experience. As I followed Stephen out of the Paddock in a sort of equestrian trance, I caught sight of his father's face, pale and fixed in its most strenuous expression ; his eyes followed his son, on whose departure he was too intent to be able to take in anyone else. We filed through a gate under some trees : " Gentleman George " was standing by the gate : he stared up at me as I passed. " That's the 'oss for my money," was all that he said, but his measured tone somehow brought me to my senses, and I was able to look about me when we got down to the starting place. But even then I was much more a passenger than a resolute rider with his wits about him to " pinch " a good start. There were seven others, I kept close to Stephen. We lined up uneasily ; while the starter (on his dumpy grey cob) was instructing us to keep the red flags on the right and the white flags on the left (which we already knew) I noticed Pomfret, (on a well-bred, excitable brown) and Brownrigg (Croplady's bright chestnut looking very compact) already stealing forward on the side furthest from him. When he said " Go " I went with the others, albeit with no sense of initiative. The galloping hoofs sounded strange. But Cockbird felt strong under me and he flicked over the first fence with level and unbroken stride ; he was such a big jumper and so quick over his fences that I had to pull him back after each one in order to keep level with Jerry, who was going his best pace all the way. One of the soldiers (in a top-hat) was making the running with Brownrigg and Pomfret close behind him. At the awkward fifth fence (the one on a bank) Pomfret's horse jumped sideways and blundered as he landed ; this caused Pomfret to address him in uncomplimentary language, and at the next obstacle (another awkward one) he ran out to the left, taking one of the soldiers with him. This, to my intense relief, was the last I saw of him. I took it in a place where a hole had been knocked in it in the previous races. The next thing I remember was the brook, which had seemed wide and intimidating when I was on foot and had now attracted a small gathering of spectators. But, water-jumps are deceptive things and Cockbird shot over this one beautifully : (Stephen told me afterwards that he'd " never seen a horse throw such an enormous lep "). We went on up a long slope of firm pasture-land, and I now became aware of my responsibility ; my arms were aching and my fingers were numb and I found it increasingly difficult to avoid taking the lead, for after jumping a couple more fences and crossing a field of light ploughland we soared over a hedge with a big drop and began to go down the other side of the hill. Jerry was out-paced and I was level with Mikado and the Cavalry soldier who had been cutting out the work. As Stephen dropped behind he said, " Go on, George ; you've got 'em stone-cold." We were now more than three parts of the way round, and there was a sharp turn left-handed where we entered on the last half-mile of the course. I lost several lengths here by taking a wide sweep round the white flag, which Brownrigg almost touched with his left boot. At the next fence the soldier went head over heels, so it was just as well for me that I was a few lengths behind him. He and his horse were still rolling about on the ground when I landed well clear of them. Brownrigg looked round and then went steadily on across a level and rather wet field which compelled me to take my last pull at Cockbird. Getting on to better ground, I remembered Mr. Gaffikin's advice, and let my horse go after him. When I had drawn up to him it was obvious that Cockbird and Mikado were the only ones left in it. I was alone with the formidable Brownrigg. The difference between us was that he was quite self-contained and I was palpitating with excitement.

We were side by side: approaching the fourth fence from the finish he hit his horse and went ahead; this caused Cockbird to quicken his pace and make his first mistake in the race by going too fast at the fence. He hit it hard and pecked badly; Brownrigg, of course, had steadied Mikado for the jump after the quite legitimate little piece of strategy which so nearly caused me to "come unstuck." Nearly, but not quite. For after my arrival at Cockbird's ears, his recovery tipped me half-way back again and he cantered on across the next field with me clinging round his neck. At one moment I was almost in front of his chest. I said to myself, "I *won't* fall off," as I gradually worked my way back into the saddle. My horse was honestly following Mikado, and my fate depended on whether I could get into the saddle before we arrived at the next fence. This I just succeeded in doing, and we got over somehow. I then regained my stirrups and set off in urgent pursuit. After that remarkable recovery of mine, life became lyrical, beautified, ecstatic, or anything else you care to call it. To put it tersely, I just galloped past Brownrigg, sailed over the last two fences, and won by ten lengths.

SIEGFRIED SASSOON: *Memoirs of a Fox-Hunting Man.*

FLAT RACING

A SHEETED regiment of racers, with their saddle-bags on their backs, and their tiny grooms at their heads, marching in Indian file, on their way to a meeting, is a sight which is rare in these railway days.

THE DRUID : *Post and Paddock*, 1856.

The jockeys, too, rode from race-course to race-course with their saddle-bags at their sides and their light saddles round their waists. Sometimes nearly 100 miles in a day.

Independently of seeing him run, amateur admirers of the race-horse have here a fine opportunity of studying him in the highest state of his perfection. We allude to the place called the Warren, in which the Derby and Oaks horses are saddled and mounted. It is a small but picturesque bit of ground in the forest style, enclosed by a wall, and entered by all who choose to pay a shilling. To some it is a great treat to see the Newmarket jockeys, who may be known to them only by name. A view of half the aristocracy of England, also, is, even in these times, worth a shilling to many. The sporting men, meanwhile reap much advantage from their anxious inspection of the horses as they walk round the rural circus. They can closely observe the condition of their favourites ; and should anything dissatisfy them, they have a chance to hedge *something* before the race is run, although the ring is generally broken up a short time after the horses are assembled in the Warren.

But what is the sight in the Warren, interesting as it really is—thousands on thousands depending on the result, ruinous perhaps to many—compared with the start for the race ? Fancy twenty-four three-year colts, looking like six-year-old horses, with the bloom of condition on their coats, drawn up in a line at the starting place, with the picked jockeys of all England on their backs, and on the simple fact of which may prove the best, perhaps a million sterling depends. They are *off* ! " No, no,"—cries one jockey, whose horse turned his tail to the others just as the word " Go " was given. It is sufficient : 'tis no start : " *Come back* " roars the starter. Some are pulled up in a few hundred yards—others go twice as far. But look at that chestnut colt—white jacket and black cap—with thousands depending upon him ! He is three parts of the way to Tattenham's corner before his rider can restrain him. Talk of agonising moments ! the pangs of death ! what can at all equal these ? but there are no winnings without losings, and it is *nuts* to those who have backed him out. Who can say, indeed, but that, his temper being known, the false start may have been *contrived* to accommodate him ? However, they are all back again at the post, and each rider endeavouring to be more well placed. Observe the cautious John Day, how quietly he manœuvres to obtain an inside location for his worthy master, his Grace of Grafton. Look at neat little Arthur Pavis patting his horse on the neck and sides, and admiring himself at the same time ; but his breeches and boots are really good. Watch Sam Chifney minutely ; but first and foremost his seat in the saddle——

" Incorpsed and demi-natured
With the brave beast——"

and his countenance ! 'tis calm, though thoughtful. But he has much to think of; he and his confederates have thousands on the race, and he is now running it in his mind's eye. Harry Edwards and Robinson are side by side, each heavily backed to win. How they are formed to ride! Surely Nature must have a mould for a jockey for the purpose of displaying her jewel, the horse. And that elegant horseman Sam Day; but see how he is wasted to bring himself to the weight! Observe the knuckles of his hands and the patellae of his knees, how they appear almost breaking through the skin! But if he have left nearly half of his frame in the sweaters, the remaining half is full of vigour; and we'll answer for it his horse don't find him wanting in the struggle. Then that slim young jockey, with high cheek bones and long neck, in the green jacket and orange cap—surely he must be in a *galloping consumption.* There is a pallid bloom on his sunken cheek, rarely seen but on the face of death, and he wants but the grave-clothes to complete the picture. Yet we need not fear; he is heart-whole and well: but having had short notice, has lost fifteen pounds in the last forty-eight hours. *They are off again!* a beautiful start and a still more beautiful sight! All the hues of the rainbow in the colours of the riders and complexions of their horses! What a spectacle for the sportsmen, who take their stand on the hill on the course to see the first part of the race, and to observe the places their favourites have gotten; they are all in a cluster, the jockeys glancing at each other's horses, for they cannot do more in such a crowd. They are soon, however, a little more at their ease: the severity of the ground, and the rapidity of the pace, throw the soft-hearted ones behind and at Tattenham's corner there is room for observation. "I think I can win," says Robinson to himself, "if I can but continue to live with my horses; for I know I have the speed of all here. But I must take a strong pull down to this hill, for we have not been coming over Newmarket flat." Pavis's horse is going sweetly, and the Yorkshireman, Scott, lying well up. But where is Chifney? Oh! like Christmas, *he's coming*, creeping up in his usual form, and getting the blind side of Harry Edwards. Chapple is here on a dangerous horse,* and John Day with a strain of old Prunella. *It is a terrible race!* There are seven in front within the distance, and nothing else has a chance to win. The set-to begins; they are all good ones. Whips are at work—and people shout—hearts throb—ladies faint—the favourite is beat—white jacket with black cap wins.

Now a phalanx of cavalry descends the hill towards the grand-stand, with "Who has won?" in each man's mouth.

NIMROD: *The Turf*, 1852.

* The above was written in the year 1833, when Mr. Sadler's Dangerous ridden by James Chapple was favourite for the Derby, which he won. Chapple also won the Oaks in the same year.

The Signal for the start being given, put him on at near three-quarter speed, or if his strength will allow it, more, but be sure you put him not to more than he is able to perform, hold the Reins pretty strait in your hand, but by no means check him in his Course, but let him run chearfully, and give him all the encouragement you can, and so let him run the whole Race through. If you, during the Course, find his strength to fail him, or that he begins to yield, give him what ease you can, and do not force him to too great a swiftness but use him so he may be at all times well pleased with his courses and free to run, and so in a short time you will bring him to perfection, but if he be anyway discouraged at first, he will never perform according to your Expectation.

Now the next thing material to be observed is, upon what ground you run, and then consider which ground your Horse takes most Delight to run upon, for this may turn to your great advantage, the which you may best take notice of in his Heats or in his First Race, whether it be smooth, rough, dry, wet, or a little rising that he most eagerly covets, and for the future chuse it if possible in all your Races.

When the Race is ended, wherein if he have been exceeding hard put to it, by no means let him stand still but gallop him moderately about some green Field, the better to let him take breath by degrees and cool accordingly, the which when you find he has pretty well done, have him into some dry gravel pit or some other deep place out of the Wind, or if these be more convenient, then to the thickest Bushes, or trees you can meet with, and there having his Cloths ready, with a large blunt Knife or some old piece of Iron or Wood, flat like a Ruler, yet having a blunt edge, scrape the sweat off from his Body ; laying the strength of both your Hands to the same till none appear in any part, and between whiles give your Horse a turn or two, and then scrape him again till he has done sweating at which time pull off his Saddle and scrape the place on which it was ; likewise then with dry Cloths, rub him in all parts, not omitting any place, exceeding well, put on his Cloths and girt his Saddle on upon them, immediately after which, you must gallop him gently for a considerable space, then rub him slightly, not taking off his Cloths especially from his Head and Neck ; then you may alight and walk him in your Hand about the Heath or Field, but be sure you suffer him not to graze if he should offer it, and when you perceive him cool and dry, ride him home gently ; you may gallop him softly if you please.

Attributed to GERVASE MARKHAM : *The Complete Jockey*, 17th Century.

A TRIAL—TWENTIETH CENTURY

By the middle or end of March a good many of the early two-year-olds should be fit to try out. *And now comes the exciting part of a trainer's life.* Now he knows whether any of his geese are swans, or whether, as is usually the case, most of his swans are geese. The two-year-old that hitherto was regarded with little favour, when tried, now beats the lot, whilst those that as yearlings looked like catching swallows and aeroplanes, after covering three furlongs, begin to go backwards, and as we say "anybody can have them."

Perhaps the most exciting trial I have seen was when I first jumped off The Tetrarch. I had three in that gallop, a couple of two-year-olds that I knew went a bit, and an old horse that was giving away 21 lb. As this was the first time that The Tetrarch had been really jumped off I told the boy who was riding him to lie beside the others, and, when he commenced to tire, to ease him up. Imagine my surprise to see, after three furlongs, the old horse and the speedy two-year-olds hard-ridden, but The Tetrarch, two lengths ahead of the rest, and still going at apparently half-speed. The boy on his back was sitting quite still and doing nothing to urge his mount forward, though the others were all out.

H. S. Persse: "Training," *Flat Racing*, Lonsdale Library.

As a two-year-old he won all his seven races, total value £22,500, slamming all opponents. Before the flat-racing season of 1913 had run half its course the grey "Rocking Horse" was a public idol, as he and Steve Donoghue, who rode him in all his races went down to the start they were cheered all the way by the admiring crowds. His speed was terrific, and his personality and size amazing; he looked like a furnished five-year-old. So great was his popularity that the Kempton Park executive announced in the advertisements of the Meeting there on 10th October 1913, that he was to run in the Imperial Produce Plate; no other case can be recalled of an individual horse being mentioned in an advertisement of a race meeting. The grey did not run, he had hit himself at exercise a few days before. He never ran again.—P. B.

The following appeared in *The Times* shortly afterwards:

The Tetrarch was struck out of the Derby at 10.48 a.m. yesterday morning.

Mr. H. S. Persse, the trainer of Captain McCalmont's famous grey colt, sent the following telegram to the Press Association yesterday:—

Having received information from my head man at Stockbridge after racing yesterday that Tetrarch's leg had filled subsequent to his gallop on Tuesday, and having ascertained later more fully extent of the injury, I wired to Captain McCalmont, who is out training with his regiment in Ireland, advising him to scratch the horse for the Derby, and I take the earliest opportunity of making this public through the Press Association.

CAVALRY RIDING

"If doughty deeds my lady please
Right soon I'll mount my steed."
James Grahame.

At no time have more glorious deeds been done by cavalry than were achieved by the Prussian horsemen of those days, Frederick the Great and his cavalry generals Zeithen and Seidlitz in the battles of Strigau, Kesseldorf, Roszbach, 1757, Leuthen and Zorndorf 1758.

Their arm was the sword ; their trust lay in the individual powers and good riding of their horsemen ; their tactics consisted in speed and determination. Seidlitz practised his hussars at going across country, using their swords and firearms at speed ; and various were the feats to which he drilled his men, in order to make them expert in the management of their horses and arms. One of these was riding in at speed between the arms of a windmill while it was working. This feat Seidlitz often performed himself after he had attained the rank of a general officer.

The horsemen of Frederick the Great, who held in large numbers, till the opportunity offered or necessity required them to be let loose, then burst over the battle-ground, and swept down all in their impetuous course ; the word on their hearts, as well as lips, being " Charge home ! "

The Prussian cavalry were ordered to shout and make as much noise as possible when attacking infantry to prevent their hearing the whistling of the bullets ; but when charging cavalry the deepest silence was preserved, and all hung in breathless suspense on the word of command which was to hurl them simultaneously on the foe.

The Russian infantry, at the battle of the Trebia in 1799, were charged by the French cavalry when in line ; they fired during the advance to the last moment, lay down, and, letting the French horse pass over them, got up and gave them a volley that emptied many a saddle.

CAPT. L. F. NOLAN : *Cavalry ; the History and Tactics*, 1853.
(The ill-fated Nolan of Balaclava.)

" Armour protects the wearer, and prevents him from injuring others."
Attributed to one of the German Emperors.

As fair a test of the relative efficiency of men in armour and those without is to be found in the charges and conflicts of cavalry at Waterloo. Our men had no armour, they were overmatched greatly in numbers, yet when they charged they drove the cuirassiers before them ; and as for single combatants, if we take the Life Guardsman Shaw, we have a fair proof of the superiority of the man unencumbered with armour : it is said he killed several of his steel-clad opponents in fair fight, and when set upon by four of them at once, he killed three, and was then disabled by a pistol-shot from the fourth. Captain Siborne thus describes a charge of cavalry at Waterloo :

"They are the far-famed cuirassiers of France, led on by Kellermann ; gallant spirits that have hitherto overcome the finest troops that could be brought against them, and have grown grey in glory. Trumpets sound the charge ; in the next instant your ears catch the low thundering noises of their horses' hoofs, and your breathless excitement is wound to the highest pitch, as the adverse lines dash together with a shock which at the moment you expect must end in their mutual annihilation. Observe the British how they seem to doubt for a second in what manner to deal with their opponents. Now they urge their powerful steeds into the intervals between the necks of those of the cuirassiers. Swords, brandished high in air, gleam fitfully in rapid succession throughout the lines ; here clashing together, there clanging against helmet and cuirass, which ring under their redoubted strokes. See, the struggle is but a moment doubtful ; the cuirassiers, *seemingly* encumbered by their coats of mail are yielding to superior strength, dexterity and bravery combined ; men and horses reel and stagger to the earth ; gaps open out in their line ; numbers are backing out, others are failing turning round ; their whole line now turns and breaks asunder into fragments : in the next moment they appear, as if by a miracle, to be swept off the crest of the position, and being closely and hotly pursued by the victors, the whole, rushing down the other side of the ridge, are snatched from your view."

Sergeant-Major Cotton relates the following encounter :

"A hussar and a cuirassier had got entangled in the mêlée, and met in the plain in full view of our line ; the hussar was without a cap and bleeding from a wound in the head that did not hinder him from attacking his steel-clad adversary. He soon proved that the strength of cavalry consists in good horsemanship and the skilful use of the sword, and not in being clad in heavy defensive armour. The superiority of the hussar was visible the moment their swords crossed ; after a few wheels, a tremendous facer made the Frenchman reel in his saddle, and all his attempts to escape his more active foe became unavailing ; a second blow stretched him on the ground, amidst the cheers of the light horseman's comrades, the third German hussars who were ardent spectators of the combat."

COTTON : *A Voice from Waterloo.*

General Morand, a French officer in the Napoleonic Wars, writing of the Russian Don Cossacks after their complete defeat of almost double their strength of French cavalry at Mühlberg in 1813 says :

" But these rude horsemen are ignorant of our *divisions,* of our *regular alignments,* of all that *order* which we so *overweeningly* estimate. Their custom is to keep their horse close between their legs ; their feet rest in broad stirrups, which support them when they use their arms. They spring from a state of rest to the full gallop, and at that gallop they make a dead halt : their horses second their skill, and seem only part of themselves ; these men are always on the alert, they move with extraordinary rapidity, have few wants, and are full of warlike ardour. What a magnificent spectacle was that of the French cavalry flashing in gold and steel under the rays of a June sun, extending its lines upon the flanks of the hills of the Niemen, and burning with eagerness and courage ! What bitter reflections are those of the ineffectual manœuvres which exhausted it against the Cossacks, those irregular forces until then so despised, but which did more for Russia than all the regular armies of that Empire ! Every day they were to be seen on the horizon, extended over an immense line, whilst their daring flankers came and braved us even in our ranks. We formed and marched against this line, which, the moment we reached it, vanished, and the horizon no longer showed anything but birch trees and pines ; but an hour afterwards, whilst our horses were feeding, the attack was resumed, and a black line again presented itself ; the same manœuvres were resumed, which were followed by the same result. It was thus that the finest and bravest cavalry exhausted and wasted itself against men whom it deemed unworthy of its valour."

General Sir Charles Shaw in a letter published in the *Morning Chronicle* in Nov. 1853 gives an account by a Prussian officer of Circassian Cavalry :

" The Circassian wears a pointed steel helmet, with a long horse-tail pendant from it ; a net of steelwork hangs down from the lower part of the helmet, protects the front and nape of the neck, and is looped together under the chin, underneath a short red vest, cut in the Polish fashion. He is clad in a species of coat-of-mail, consisting of small bright rings of steel intervened ; his arms, from the wrist to the elbow, and his legs, from the foot of the shin-bone to the knee, are guarded by thin plates of steel ; he also wears close pantaloons and laced boots. Two long Turkish pistols, as well as a poniard (small dagger), are stuck into his girdle, he has a leather strap with a noose, like a Mexican lasso, hanging at his side, which he throws with great dexterity over the head of his enemy : a Turkish sabre and a long Turkish musket are slung behind his back, and two cartridge-holders across his breast. The skill with which the Circassians use their weapons is really beyond belief. I have seen them repeatedly fire at a piece of card lying on the ground, at full speed, without ever missing. They will pick up a piece of money from the ground while executing a charge, by bending themselves round below the horse's belly, and, after seizing the piece, suddenly throw themselves back into the saddle. They form the choicest body of cavalry in the Turkish service, and I have watched them, when charging, attack their opponents with a sabre in each hand, managing their reins with their mouths ; they will spring out of their saddles, take aim and fire from behind their horses, then jump into their saddles again, wheel round, and reload their guns as they retreat in full career. They are perfect madmen in the attack, and few troops would withstand the utter recklessness of danger they evince."

The Circassians, who were inhabitants of the West Caucasus, resisted Russian domination for thirty years, after being surrendered by Turkey to Russia by the treaty of Adrianople in 1829.

They were unsurpassed in the management of their war-horses and arms, and so proud of their skill, that, whereas most nations showed wounds received in action as honourable scars, the Circassians hid theirs as silent witnesses of their awkwardness and want of address in single combat.—P. B.

Extract from a report, " Defects, Civil and Military, of the Indian Government " : by Lt.-Gen. Sir Charles Napier, G.C.B., in 1850.

" The hardships of war are by our dressers of cavalry thought too little for the animals' strength ; they add a bag with the Frenchified name of 'valise,' containing an epitome of a Jew's old-clothes shop. Notably so if the regiment be hussars, a name given to Hungarian light horsemen, remarkable for activity, and carrying no other *baggage* than a small axe and a tea-kettle to every dozen men. Our hussars' old-clothes bag contains jackets, breeches of all dimensions, drawers, snuff-boxes, stockings, pink boots, yellow boots, eau-de-cologne, Windsor soap, brandy, satin waistcoats, cigars, kid gloves, tooth-brushes, hair-brushes, dancing spurs ; and thus, a *light* cavalry horse carries 21 stone. Hussars our men are not ; a real hussar, including his twelfth part of a kettle, does not weigh twelve stone—before he begins plundering. The heavy cavalry horse, strange to say, carries less than the light cavalry—only twenty stone ! A British regiment of cavalry on parade is a beautiful sight ; give it six months' hard work in the field, and while the horses fail the men lose confidence ; the vanity of dress supersedes efficiency. Take eight or ten stone off the weight carried, and our cavalry will be the most efficient in the world."

A RECRUITING POSTER DATED 1803

A HORSE. A HORSE. My kingdom for a horse.

Now, my lads, for the 14th Light Dragoons or the Duchess of York's Own.

All you who are kicking your heels behind a solitary desk with too little wages, and a pinch-gut Master—

All you with too much wife, or are perplexed with obstinate and unfeeling parents may apply to

Sergeant Hammond, Rose and Crown, Whitechapel.

You are quartered in the fertile county of Kent, where you have provisions remarkably cheap, luxurious living to the brave and ambitious mind is but a secondary object, else thousands would repair to the standard of the gallant 14th, could they

obtain the honour of being received.

Those of address and education are sure of preferment, your comforts in this service surpass all clerks and mechanics, an hospitable table and capacious bowl of punch that will float or

sink the little Corsican Chief.

N.B.—Four Farriers are wanted and a Master for the Band.

GOD SAVE THE KING

Happily, the horse is no longer subjected to the horrors of the battlefield, in the British Army at any rate. Unhappily, at the same time he is no longer called upon to give us the added thrill and magnificence to ceremonial occasions, or at least only in a very limited degree, for now only one squadron of the Life Guards still have their horses which they share with the Royal Horse Guards when on ceremonial duty. To these must be added the King's Troop Royal Horse Artillery. It was they who fired the royal salute of 41 guns in Hyde Park on the memorable occasion of the birth of Prince Charles of Edinburgh on 14th Nov. 1948.—P. B.

The King's Troop Royal Horse Artillery.

POLO

For the daring turn and the skilful stroke,
  The ever-quickening stride,
The ring of the stirrup, the clash of the stick,
  And the rush of the furious ride ;
The cheer when the ball through the goal is driven
  By the steady hand and eye,
Have a wild delight in themselves alone
  That can never grow old or die.

H. C. Bentley.

Present-day polo is almost a different game to that which Kipling describes so beautifully in his classic story *The Maltese Cat,* first published in 1898. The neat little grey, with the rest of his illustrious team mates, was under fourteen hands high. There was a height limit in those days, differing in each of the three polo-playing countries of the world; in England the limit was 14 hands, in India 13 hands 3 inches, and in America 14 hands 1 inch. In the beginning of this century the limit in England was raised to 14 hands 2 inches, as it was found almost impossible to obtain a sufficient supply of ponies of fourteen hands. There was then also an off-side rule. Neither of these restrictions exists to-day. The memory of the American team which came over here for the Westchester Cup matches in 1936 brings back the vision of their magnificent ponies—Winston Guest's string—more like middle-weight hunters than polo ponies, some of them sixteen hands, clean bred, and like the beautiful chestnut mare Lady Newberry, winners on the flat. Michael Phipps too—the chestnut Tarara which he played in a bitless bridle, and his famous lop-eared grey, Brown Fern. Racers, fit, and schooled to perfection. No wonder then that modern polo is the fastest game in the world. No "football," "scrimmages" and "tap-tappings" as The Maltese Cat played, but long clean hits, up and down and across the ground, the ball never coming to rest but met and hit clean and true on the bounce, full toss, or half volley. At the pace and toughness of the modern game it would be difficult to imagine, say, Mr. Gerald Balding, playing a chukker of an international match with one arm only, like Lutyens on The Maltese Cat after he had broken his collar bone in a fall.

The game of polo perhaps more than any other combines all man's finest qualities, nerve, endurance, fitness, strength, self-control, anticipation, team spirit, dash, quickness of hand, eye and brain, and above all horsemanship, which means understanding and sympathy with one's pony which Whyte Melville describes so well in *Riding Recollections*:—P. B.

"... surely your first duty is to the gallant and generous animal that would never *fail* you at your need, but would gallop till his heart broke, for your mere amusement and caprice.

"Of all our relations with the dumb creation, there is none in which man has so entirely the best of it as the one-sided partnership that exists between the horse and his rider."

The neat little grey, with the rest of his illustrious team mates.

With one arm only, like Lutyens on The Maltese Cat.

PIGSTICKING

. . . I'LL fill my cup, and drink it up
To Saddle, Spur, and Spear.

God gave the horse for man to ride
And steel wherewith to fight,
And wine to swell his soul with pride
And women for delight;
But a better gift than all these four
Was when he made the fighting boar!

India is not a fox-hunting spot,
But we make the best of what we have got,
And the best of all sports in that far far land
Is a boar in front and a spear in hand.

Chorus.

Over the valley, over the level,
Thro' the dâk jungle, ride like the devil;
There's a nullah in front—there's a boar as well,
Sit down in your saddle and ride like hell.

Pigsticking Song.

THE KADIR CUP

The Kadir Cup has often been described, but I must try and write a little about it and give you a few notes. For I hunted the country seven seasons, and have ridden in it fourteen years.

"The blue riband of pigsticking," the meeting lasts three days, and is always held in the end of March. It begins on Monday. The heats are drawn on Sunday evening. It is good to get out early, to go round the 120 to 150 horses that are running, and to meet old friends. The line next morning is a fine sight, with 50 elephants crowded with spectators, and a fair sprinkling of ladies. In front is the line of 150 coolies, with the flag elephant, signallers, and the shikaries on their camels.

Ahead are the three heats with their umpires—I quote from a description of my mother's: "Well worth a study are many of the competitors, men from all parts of India, of all branches and professions. Here is clearly distinguishable a veteran, his good horse marked with scars perhaps, honourable mementoes of the chase, nursing the umpire, riding in his pocket as it were, to get the best of the start. There is a youngster fidgeting and prancing, showing the strain on horse and rider; here, again, a well-known cross-country rider on a blood steeplechaser; and so on with endless variety.

"All stand still until a wave of the master's hand causes the line to advance, in a silence broken only by the swish of the beaters' sticks and the passage of the elephants through the golden, waving grass and thick green bushes. A sudden shout proclaims that a boar has broken, and that the heat nearest can be seen following their umpire in pursuit. When satisfied that all see the pig, and that it is rideable, down goes the flag, and faint on the breeze comes the thrilling word 'Ride.' Meantime the halted line follows, with deep interest and raised glasses, the fortune of the chase. The leader's quick start and gallant ride, the desperate efforts of those behind, the sudden jink, the neck-and-neck race with the second man, another jink, a horse down perhaps, and then—the spear; one man pulling up and showing his spear for blood to the umpire, the others riding on to kill.

"And last, and by no means least, comes the suspense while the umpire signals to the flag elephant, visible everywhere, the number of the winner; the flag elephant then hoists the winner's number according to the printed programme, and the line goes on at once.

"Thus it continues through heat after heat until a rest is called for luncheon. We had started at 7 a.m., and I think no one is sorry to find some refreshment ready for us under a big tree by a stream in a picturesque spot; and I am sure we all enjoy our lunch and rest. Very soon, however, we are remounting our elephants, and have a long and exciting afternoon, which does not end until 7.30."

A long day's work, I always admire the keen ladies who one and all stick it out. They are most welcome at this meeting. The second day is a repetition of the first, but with less heats to run off and shorter hours.

On the Wednesday are run off the semi-finals and final, when we congratulate the winner on an envied and deserved success. In the afternoon are the Horse and Pony Hog Hunters' Cups, point to point races over several miles of pigsticking country. Grief is common, but our doctor and vet. ride behind, and all is well. So with speeches, dinner, and songs another Kadir Cup is over.

GENERAL SIR ALEXANDER WARDROP: *Modern Pigsticking*, 1914.

The voices of the Kadir that sound so sweet and strong,
How vivid are the pictures, how thick the vision's throng.
Who shall describe the beauty, the magic of them all
In silent hours when memory's powers those happy days recall?

The sudden jink.

RIDING FOR LADIES

THERE is such a pleasure and gratification in riding, and riding well, that the young, especially with hale constitutions, are quite fascinated with the practice; and really their horses, when mounted, as we often see them, by elegant women, seem to vie with the conscious satisfaction they occasion with their fair riders.

JOHN ADAMS, RIDINGMASTER: *Analysis of Horsemanship*, 1799.

Richard I, 1189–1199

In the reign of this prince Side-ſaddles were firſt known in England, as it will appear from the following anecdote; and although it is mixed with other particulars, which do not immediately relate to the ſubject, I venture to give the paragraph entire, as it is to be found in F. Roffi Antiquarii Warwicein. Hiſt. Rerum Ang., in Latin. In English it may be rendered thus: "In his days alſo began the deteſtable cuſtom of wearing long pointed ſhoes, faſtened with chains of ſilver and ſometimes of gold, up to the knees. Likewiſe noble ladies then uſed high heads and cornets, and robes with long trains, and *Seats or Side-ſaddles* on their horſes, by the example of the reſpectable Queen Ann, daughter of the King of Bohemia, who firſt introduced this cuſtom into this Kingdom: for *before* women of every rank rode as men do, with their legs aſtride the backs of their horſes."

Thus far our Warwick Hiſtorian; and it is certain that this was not the uſual way of riding till about this time; for Nicetas, of the Byzantine hiſtorians, who wrote an hiſtory of 1118, to the year 1205, ſays, that at this period, women did not ride as they used to do, ſitting on a Side-ſaddle, but mounted their horſes with their legs *indecently aſtride*. Thus Side-ſaddles appear to have been used many centuries ago, and before the female ſex took up the faſhion of riding like men, for which they are reprehended by the Greek hiſtorian: and hard indeed is the *equestrian* situation of the ſex! for if they are to be accused of indelicacy for riding after the *manner of men*, they certainly hazard their ſafety too much in riding after the *manner of women*.

Richard Berenger, Eſq.,
Gentleman of the Horse to HIS MAJESTY.

The History and Art of Horsemanship, 1771.

The side-saddle is supposed to have been invented by Catherine de Medici (1519–1589, wife of King Henry II of France), and Brantome in his *Memoires* written just after the death of his patroness gives as her feminine motive:

"The desire to show her leg was one reason for the invention, because she had very nice ones, her calves being well-formed, and she took pleasure in well-booting herself, and seeing that her *chausse* were well put on and not wrinkled."

"Ar wouldn't be a woman's hoss a' nowt."

R. S. SURTEES : *James Pigg.*

LADY'S SEAT :

Except as regards the legs a lady should sit on a saddle exactly like a man. For some time there has been talk of ladies riding astride, which practice would deprive her of all feminine grace, and would afford no useful result. The great want in man's seat is firmness, which would be still more difficult for a woman to acquire if she rode in a cross-saddle, because her thighs are rounder and weaker than those of a man. Discussion of this subject is therefore useless. Ladies who ride astride get such bad falls that they soon give up this practice. . . .

A horsewoman should have great pliability of body which she will acquire by practice in riding and other preliminary exercises, of which dancing is the best. It also depends on certain small details of dress, about which I may give the following advice. . . .

I strongly advise that she should wear socks instead of stockings ; because a garter is always inconvenient and may cause serious wounds. The socks should be furnished with a close fitting collar of some soft and elastic material, such as knitting or jersey, lined with silk, or, still better, very fine doeskin. The trousers should be strapped with india-rubber and should fit rather closely, so that they may not wrinkle. The boots should have elastic sides and not buttons, which might cause wounds. I prefer ordinary boots to long boots, which are too hard, and are consequently apt to cut the wearer under the knee, and to prevent her feeling the horse with her leg. The corset should be very short and low. A long busk is not only inconvenient, but is also dangerous. I would not have touched on these details but for the fact that the dress of the horsewoman is closely connected with strength of seat and ease in the saddle. I have seen so many ladies returning from a ride in pain, and condemned to spend many days in a long chair, that I am certain that the points to which I have drawn attention are important. The head-dress of the lady should be firmly arranged, so that it may not occupy her attention in which case she will think too little of her horse. Then, if she loses her hat, she will probably lose her head.

JAMES FILLIS : *Breaking and Riding*, 1911.

Caption *vide* illustrated sporting periodical : "The last fence in the ladies' race at the Old Flurry & Blastow Point to Point. Miss Diana Modern-Miss, aged seventeen (without cap) was the winner of this event riding her own horse 'Nowadays.' She had a similar success last week at the Forlock Vale fixture."

THE wide world for a Kingdom,
And the saddle for a throne!
WILL. H. OGILVIE.

Exmoor the riding playground of England
CECIL ALDIN.

. . . the tiny brown streams were singing their song.

Through heather and woodland, through meadow and lea,
We flow from the forest away to the sea.
In cloud and in vapour, in mist and in rain,
We fly from the sea to the forest again.
Oh ! dear is the alder and dearer the fern,
And welcome are kingfisher, ousel and herne,
The swan from the tide-way, the duck from the mere,
But welcome of all is the wild Red-Deer.

HON. J. W. FORTESCUE : *The Story of a Red-Deer*, 1904.

"HOBSON'S CHOICE"

Thomas Hobson, born in 1544, is said to have been the first who let out horses for hire. From his extensive and well-run business in Cambridge he had amassed a fortune before he died in 1631.

Hobson kept, as the Cambridge story goes, a number of horses for hire in his long stable. The rule was that one, and that one only, which stood nearest the door, should be the first sent out. This one or none you might take—each should so get its due rest. This condition held good, to be infringed by no single University man. The nearest horse to the door was the nearest to the road. Why has this sensible mode of choice not been preserved? Why was such a good rule ever abolished? Remember, oh Cambridge, to renew Hobson's old rule, and you shall see horses again like his.

VINCENT BOURNE, 1730.

DAWN IN THE HORSE PADDOCK

A recollection recaptured from a decade in Australia.

It is still dark as we take the path to the stable with saddle and bridle on arm. Barbette moves restlessly in her box and whinnies softly as we draw the bolt. Usually some quiet old slave of a stock-horse fills the role of "night horse," and is kept in for running up the horses, but Barbette is being trained for the local races, and as an early morning canter in the paddock does her no harm and gives her an appetite for her breakfast oats, she, for the time being, is available—in reliable hands.

She faces up to the bridle with a little snort of pretended fear, hunches her back as the cold girth nips her, and steps out into the dark as nimbly as if she were going down to the starting post.

"Steady, Barbette!" and we swing into the saddle. She gives a plunge or two in sheer joy of freedom, and then walks off at a quick bridle-slapping gait. It is over two miles to the farthest point of the horse paddock, and we take the well-defined path, beaten out by many hoofs, down which the mob comes each morning to the stock-yard. It is still too dark to gather horses with any certainty, so we move slowly on, first across a bit of open plain, then through a patch of buddah bush, and out into the open again over a big box-flat. A whinny to our right betrays the presence of horses, and a little farther on we pass some more, their dim forms faintly discernible in the starlight. Some horse-bells sound far away to the left; those, we know, are on the waggon-horses. We cross a small sandhill covered with low scrub, and follow the path through a clump of thick sapling pine, and then emerge on a big plain, an expanse of rich girth-deep barley grass with lignum bushes scattered here and there.

A faint streak of grey lightens the eastern sky, and Barbette lifts her lean head and whinnies to the dawn. Here a mob of ten or twelve horses is feeding, busily tugging at the long, lush grass. We pull up for a moment and watch them; they scarcely lift their heads, as though they knew well that they have only a few minutes more before they will be hurried off to a long hungry day under the saddle.

The light broadens, and now we can see the shimmering line of wire fence which marks the boundary of the paddock. No need to go farther out. Moving beyond the little mob of feeding horses we uncoil our stock-whip, fourteen foot of snake-plait, a yard of greenhide fall, and nine inches of silken cracker; the long lash falls with a thunder that reverberates in the sandhills and dies away across the river beyond the homestead.

With a rush the little mob of horses near us wheels together and races away towards the sandhill, joined by two or three others which were scattered among the lignum. Again we make the long lash roar a challenge. Barbette is excited now by the drumming hoofs. She roars and plunges, fighting for her head. "Steady, steady! Barbette!"

With a careful look round to see that we have missed nothing on this wide plain, we give the mare rein, and she swings into her stride with a squeal of delight. In front of her nearly a score of horses are on the road for home, flinging up their heels in sheer wantonness and biting playfully at each other. "Racing, is it?" Barbette seems to say to herself, as she flings her head and grips the bit, laying herself down to her strong gallop—and Barbette takes holding when she means business. If we let her go she would be up to the mob in a flash, and fighting with them for the lead, but presently she comes back to our hands, bends her neck in token of surrender, and thereafter plays with her bit like the perfect lady she is.

The horse paddock, though long, is narrow, and now that the mob is in front of us the horses gather themselves from either side, and all we have to do is to ring the whip at intervals as we follow them at a brisk canter.

One thing, however, we remember: and that is that Scotty and Comet, the old wagonette horses, are notorious for "planting"—hiding themselves in the scrub in the hope of being left behind and securing a day's idleness; so we turn off the path and search the saplings on either side. Sure enough, motionless in a thick clump, stands cunning old Scotty with his head hidden in a thick pine like an ostrich's in the sand, hoping to escape notice. A few yards away Comet stands similarly hidden. A shout conveys to them that the game is up, and they lob away into the open. Catching Barbette by the head, we sail after them, and overtaking Scotty, who is the slowest as he is the most cunning, land him a rousing cut over the rump to remind him that his sneaking little game has not gone unnoticed.

The two old reprobates join the mob, and at the same time the manager's four-in-hand team of beautiful greys come gliding through the bushes—all together as usual—Solitude, Chieftain, Viscount, and Merriment—a team famous on every western showground and winners of very many prizes.

Another old grey hobbles in from the plain—old broken-down Haphazard, once a rare good one, but now pensioned off; he persists in coming in every morning with the mob, and will not be left; and if you cut him out and try to leave him he follows on behind at a stilted trot and manages to reach the yard almost as soon as the others.

Now we pick up the heavy draught-horses, which race clumsily behind the saddle-hacks, jangling their bells and heaving their hindquarters at one another in elephantine play.

We have now some thirty horses in front of us, and assuming that none has crossed the river beyond the homestead we should have them all; so with merry music from the stock-whip in case any straggler should still be loitering on the flanks we follow on down the dusty pathway, revelling in the strong canter of Barbette, hard-held, as she marks every swing of the whip with a forward plunge, and tosses her snaffle-rings in sheer delight.

No ride is so fully satisfying and so inspiring as this early morning canter on a good horse. All this time the east has been reddening against bars of silver and opal, and now the sun rises slowly over the horizon; the magpies wake and salute the morning with a ripple of song; the light catches the fairy webs which the spiders have spun from bough to bough; the scent of the flowering buddah bushes floats up as we cross the last little sandhill; and ahead we see the glittering roofs of the homestead. Over the last bit of open country the mob races with a thunder of hoofs, plunges through the last scattered bushes, and wheels into the stock-yard, led by old Midnight and St. Clair and Sunflower—a miscellaneous collection of stock-horses, harness-horses, and heavy draughts, with poor old Haphazard lobbing painfully in the rear.

We dismount, drop the heavy rails into place, and casting an eye over the yarded mob to see that we have missed no horse that may be wanted for the day's work lead Barbette back to her stable. The sun climbs like a ball of fire over the silver roofs. Another blazing day; but we have stolen its one most lovely hour.

WILL. H. OGILVIE.

A HUNTING MORNING

Romance came out of her box, gay enough even on this warm morning. I have met Romance before, yet each time I see her it gives me a queer pick up at the heart; she is, for her sort such a perfect thing. Not made to carry much more than Willow's eight stone seven, the little mare has done that well for the last two seasons, and has won her four point-to-points and run into a place twice. Sir Richard caught his daughter's upheld boot and threw her into the saddle (a little old favourite saddle it must have been—the flaps nipped in dark below the half panel). Willow ran the single plaited rein through her fingers and walked the mare off, while Pheelan pursued her, dusting the toe of her boot with pertinacious zeal. His blue jackdaw-like eyes were everywhere, and he was full of the imperative importance of a groom on a hunting morning.

M. J. FARRELL: *Conversation Piece.*

COMING HOME FROM HUNTING

And after that it was pleasant to be riding home in the latening twilight; to hear the "chink-chink" of thrushes against the looming leafless woods and the afterglow of sunset; and to know that winter was at an end. Perhaps the old horse felt it, too, for he had settled into the rhythm of an easy striding walk instead of his customary joggle.

I can see the pair of us clearly enough; myself, with my brow-pinching bowler hat tilted on to the back of my head, staring, with the ignorant face of a callow young man, at the dusky landscape and its glimmering wet fields. And Harkaway with his three white socks caked with mud, his "goose-rump," and his little ears cocked well forward. I can hear the creak of the saddle and the clop and clink of hoofs as we cross the bridge over the brook by Dundell Farm; there is a light burning in the farmhouse window, and the evening star glitters above a broken drift of half-luminous cloud. "Only three miles more, old man," I say, slipping to the ground to walk alongside of him for a while.

It is with a sigh I remember simple moments such as those, when I understood so little of the deepening sadness of life, and only the strangeness of the spring was knocking at my heart.

SIEGFRIED SASSOON: *Memoirs of a Fox-Hunting Man.*

THE NEW FOREST

Perhaps the forest never looks so lovely as in autumn, and especially when well soaked. The heather still purpled the moor—a rich purplish-brown flecked here and there with jewel-like pools. Towards the uplands, and in the woods, the wet bracken had changed its usual autumnal orange for a rich sienna.

The forest ponies, singly or in groups, gave life and focus to the landscape.

ALLEN W. SEABY: *Skewbald.*

The Sporting Life of England!
  The Charter of the Isle!
Perish the Traitor, heart and hand,
  That would with dastard wile,
Sow discord, jealousy, or strife,
  Among the Gallant Band
Who share and shield our Sporting Life,
  The Charter of the Land.

OLD SONG.